Become A Super Salesforce Administrator

HEATHER BLACK

Published in 2025 by Discover Your Bounce Publishing

www.discoveryourbouncepublishing.com

978-1-914428-35-7

Page design and typesetting by Discover Your Bounce Publishing

REVIEWS OF THIS BOOK

"A great read, all the facts and fundamentals needed for someone making the decision to come over to Salesforce. I personally have done this course; Heather and the team have been an amazing support and got me to where I am today and I've never looked back."

Ria Field, Salesforce Administrator for Legal & General

"Become a Super Salesforce Administrator provides a comprehensive introduction to the areas you need to consider and explore as a new Salesforce admin. It's a potentially overwhelming role to step into and navigate, so this is helpful in giving you an overview of the critical items to be mindful of, and the multiple roles a Salesforce Administrator often plays."

Emma Steward, System Manager, Non-Profit

"Become a Super Salesforce Administrator is an excellent resource for new Salesforce administrators, providing a clear and practical structure for mastering the role. The book effectively outlines key responsibilities like user management, data security, and system optimisation, while offering insights into advanced areas such as AI, DevOps, and career progression. For beginners, the focus on real-world tools, step-by-step strategies, and integration of resources like AI-powered documentation tools makes it highly usable. Overall, this book is a valuable guide to becoming a confident and effective Salesforce Admin."

Srividya Pemmaraju, Certified Salesforce Administrator

"Become a Super Salesforce Admin is a must-read for anyone looking to manage their Salesforce org with confidence and clarity. I found this book helpful in providing a structured framework for key responsibilities—something that can often feel overwhelming in a busy Salesforce environment. Another standout aspect is its emphasis on business analysis, change management, and Agile project management—critical skills that admins need but don't always develop early in their careers. If you're managing a Salesforce org and want a guide to stay on top of your responsibilities, this book is a game-changer."

Clauda Tarik, Salesforce Systems Manager

CONTENTS

FOREWORD

Embarking on a new career as a Salesforce Administrator can be a daunting and exciting experience. This book will hold your hand and give you the direction you need to hit the ground running.

Your timing, by the way, is impeccable. We are in the age of agentic AI – known as the third wave of AI innovation. The way we work is transforming, with AI-powered digital teams driving business growth, boosting productivity, and enhancing human job satisfaction. As a Salesforce Administrator, you'll be at the forefront of this digital labour revolution.

You will also become a part of the Salesforce ecosystem community, providing others like you with access to skills and further training that will keep you at the forefront of innovation.

This book equips you with an action plan and guide to develop critical digital skills for the world of work in the AI-first era.

Zahra Bahrololoumi CBE, CEO of Salesforce UK and Ireland

INTRODUCTION

Would you like a structure and process for managing and developing your Salesforce CRM System?

Do you want to feel empowered to enthuse and engage your stakeholders and to deliver real results for the organisation you are working with?

If yes, then this book is for you. It will give you the insight, tools and framework to be a Super Salesforce Administrator and equip you to manage and maintain a healthy Salesforce system that keeps data secure and users happy.

In this book we walk you through the four roles and responsibilities of a Salesforce Administrator:

- The Data Champion – managing data and security
- The Change Agent – managing users
- The Problem Solver – managing the system
- The Innovator – developing the CRM Roadmap

This book will empower you to be aware of what you need to do and enable you to feel in control of your workload, managing your responsibilities effectively to ensure positive outcomes for your organisation.

Depending on the Salesforce team around you, and your existing skills, this book will guide you on how to manage tasks, learn new skills, adopt tools and give insight into career progression opportunities. From starting out as a Salesforce Administrator you will start to develop your business analysis, Agile project management, change management and development opportunity skills. From there you can set your sights on climbing the career ladder to become either a Chief Technology Officer, Salesforce Consultant, Salesforce Developer or Marketing Cloud expert. Within this book we will give you a professional development plan so you can be intentional in developing your career path to boost your earning potential and confidence.

You will enjoy being a Super Salesforce Administrator if you embrace a growth mindset and relish the learning every day.

Remember, your job is to solve problems for users and to maintain a healthy system. It's okay to not know the answers right away, but instead, it's about researching, asking for help in the forums or bringing in experts when you need them. Every day is a school day and it's about continuous learning.

I personally started my Salesforce journey in 2010, finding myself as an accidental Salesforce Administrator for my own non-profit organisation. After completing the Salesforce Administrator Training Course, I had to navigate my own path to managing the system as there was no clear instruction manual. Through my grass roots experience I decided to create better training resources for Salesforce professionals and launched Supermums in 2016 to train people as Salesforce professionals. We package a lot of added value learning and practical experience into our training programmes to equip learners with the skills they need to launch and accelerate their Salesforce career. We listen to questions, and we plug the gaps in knowledge and confidence with new resources to help learners overcome their imposter syndrome.

We find that off the shelf Salesforce Administrator training will teach you the basic admin skills but it doesn't equip you with the skills of how to manage a system and to deliver on the job of a Salesforce Administrator, so we curated this structure for you.

I first presented the 'Four Roles of an Awesome Admin' content at Dreamforce in 2019 and since then it's been refined and developed to give people the toolkit they need. It's now embellished with some amazing third-party apps that harness Artificial Intelligence (AI) to manage your system. AI tools can make your tasks much more efficient. It's definitely worth making time to learn these new tools to enhance your productivity and outcomes. I can't wait to share them with you.

To learn more about me and Supermums head to the last chapter of the book.

Throughout the book I share a suite of free resources and templates. You can use the QR code to head to the resources page on our website and download what you need.

SCAN ME

WHAT IS A SALESFORCE ADMINISTRATOR?

In this chapter we explore the role of a Salesforce Administrator and the skills you will deploy and develop depending on whether you are working as part of a team or as a solo administrator.

As a Salesforce Administrator you will focus on 'click not code' solutions. You are able to configure Salesforce relatively easily with the right training and mentoring to maintain a Salesforce CRM system on a daily basis. The starting certifications are Salesforce Administrator, Advanced Admin and App Builder and then progressing to learn other product specialisms depending on the needs of the system.

Your role is focused on developing and maintaining a system and learning the Salesforce products as required, often adopting a trainer role to help people use and manage the system.

You might be working on a support desk, be a solo administrator working in-house or building solutions as part of a Salesforce consultancy. The number in a team can also depend on the number of users.

If you are part of a team, you will typically work alongside people who conduct the business analysis, Agile project management, change management and Salesforce development. You will be led by them in terms of what to focus your time on and what to build.

If you are part of a support desk, you will respond and manage cases and help users to use and adopt the system.

If you work as a solo Salesforce Administrator you will be responsible for designing and managing requirements and you will need to develop your business analysis and Agile project management bringing in more advanced technical developer expertise as needed.

Typical Responsibilities

These are the main responsibilities of a Salesforce Administrator:

- Hands on configuration – fields, email templates, reports, automation.
- Creating training content and delivering training to users.
- Producing reports and data analytics.
- Keeping data clean and the system safe.
- Extending the CRM platform to meet new user requirements.

Business Analyst Skills

As a Salesforce Administrator you might also wear the hat of business analyst.

A business analyst invests time in understanding how the organisation and the team currently operate helping them to evaluate and improve their management processes and Key Performance Indicators (KPIs).

They facilitate conversations to elicit what the business goals are, what the pain points are, and help the team to define their future vision for management processes and performance monitoring. They will produce documentation that summarises the requirements to support the system design.

It suits someone with a passion for management consultancy who likes to improve business processes and enable the client to realise the key performance indicators that are outlined in their business plan and CRM strategy.

Typically, business analysts will have Salesforce product knowledge as well as sound business management experience. At Supermums, we recommend you undertake training in business analysis, requirements engineering and process modelling.

Typical Responsibilities

The main responsibilities of being a Salesforce business analyst include:

- Collaborating with business stakeholders to understand business processes, identify gaps within current processes, define solutions to address gaps, document user stories and business requirements and associated business value.

- Supporting the prioritisation of user stories across multiple business processes and stakeholders to drive the most business value.
- Preparing technical reports by collecting and analysing information and trends.
- Facilitating meetings and presentations to senior and c-suite stakeholders.
- Writing the business case, producing process maps, documenting requirements.

Project Manager Skills

As a Salesforce Administrator you might also wear the hat of a project manager to manage your workload.

A project manager is an expert in planning, maintaining accountability and managing resources to deliver a project successfully for a client. They enjoy being organised and using project management software to plan everything out successfully.

They will liaise and allocate team members to a project and hold the team accountable for recording time and deliverables to maintain an overview on project progress. Usually, they will report to a client/manager regularly on progress and the plan.

The project manager is measured on their success to bring a project in on time, on budget and to deliver the priority outcomes for the client. They require excellent management and people skills with an aptitude for accountability, precision and organisation.

Typically, Agile Project Management Methodology is popular in the Salesforce eco-system, but Waterfall Prince 2 Methods are still used in some cases. A technical understanding of Salesforce products is not essential as a project manager if you have a team of other technical Salesforce specialists around you, but it can be useful to have a general knowledge of what the team is delivering.

Typical Responsibilities

The main responsibilities of being a Salesforce project manager include:

- Agreeing project objectives and measures of success, including time and budget, for a Salesforce project.
- Managing, motivating and influencing team members to deliver on their tasks throughout the project life cycle.
- Identifying and mitigating potential risks and developing solutions to manage them.
- Ensuring effective use of project management software and tools by the team for managing projects.

- Building, maintaining and developing effective relationships with internal and external stakeholders.
- Planning, allocating tasks and executing the projects at hand.

Navigating the Road to Success

You will grow into the Salesforce Administrator role, developing your knowledge and suite of skills over time.

It's important to understand what is expected of you in this job role right now and to manage the expectations of people around you to make sure tasks align with your salary banding and job specification.

It's become common for more and more tasks to be added to Salesforce Administrator job specifications without the reflective job title evolution or pay increments.

Typically, Salesforce professionals with advanced technical skills, business analysis and project management skills will get paid £10k+ more than a Salesforce Administrator. It's important to know your worth and to agree a progression plan with the company you work with. See the chapter on progressing your career to help you discuss this with your line manager. We can't wait to see you flourish in your role as a Salesforce Administrator, so we will do a deep dive into the different responsibilities in the next chapter.

THE FOUR RESPONSIBILITIES OF A SALESFORCE ADMINISTRATOR

In this chapter, we delve deeper into the four responsibilities of a Salesforce Administrator.

An administrator can wear many hats, and the variety of tasks within the role can be rewarding but sometimes overwhelming if tasks are not organised and prioritised.

Being a Salesforce Administrator is an important responsibility, especially if you are in sole charge of managing a system. Your role will entail managing the CRM system and its data, keeping it secure and trusted, while also developing a system that meets the needs of the team.

To help administrators to be clear on their responsibilities we have compiled a list of 25 tasks that a Salesforce Administrator would typically need to think about when managing a system. These are categorised into four key areas of responsibility:

- The Data Champion – managing data and security
- The Problem Solver – managing the system
- The Change Agent – managers users

- The Innovator – developing the CRM Roadmap

The Data Champion - Managing Data and Security:

- Imagine yourself as the guardian of the system, protecting who has access to what and keeping the data clean and tidy.
- Considerations at a strategic level including security policies, data governance and management, user access, and password policies.
- Failure to manage data securely could result in a data breach, financial penalties, reputational risk, and, in the worst case, personal liabilities.

The Problem Solver - Managing the Health of the System:

- Imagine yourself as the housekeeper of the system, keeping the house in order by ensuring products are working effectively, errors are managed, and crucial updates are made.
- Considerations at a strategic level include a technical audit, integration, content management, and DevOps process.
- Failure to manage a system properly can result in

automation fails, customer issues, reputational risk, and user frustration.

The Change Agent - Managing User Adoption:

- Imagine yourself as the doctor of the system, triaging problems, subscribing solutions via the support desk, and supporting users to adopt the system with a range of prescriptions.
- Considerations at a strategic level include change management practices, a training strategy, and measuring user adoption.
- Failure to support users and manage change can result in low user trust and product adoption, poor customer intelligence and unusable performance management data.

The Innovator - Developing the CRM RoadMap:

- Imagine yourself as the leader of the CRM strategy where you understand the business vision and challenges and propose new technology solutions to improve efficiency and maximise ROI.
- Considerations at a strategic level include showing what's possible, demonstrating the business case, prioritising requirements, and generating buy-in.

- Failure to share product knowledge and possibilities with colleagues internally can result in multiple systems, data silos, lack of customer intelligence, poor business performance, and low value in CRM.

The Schedule of a Salesforce Administrator

One of the best approaches to managing the responsibilities is to implement a regular schedule of weekly, monthly and quarterly tasks in your diary. It's all too easy for regular routine 'boring' tasks to be forgotten in favour of new and exciting feature developments. The risk here is that while new features are being developed, the system's data could get dirty, and users lose trust in using the system. If you take your eye off the ball, the whole system can cascade.

Below is your Action Plan outlining the 25 tasks of a Salesforce Administrator:

	Daily/Weekly Tasks	**Monthly Tasks**	**Quarterly Tasks**
System Management	AI features for admin tasks	Document management	Technical Audit
	DevOps	Documenting org	Org analysis
	Error handling	Integration	Product

		management	release management
Data Management	Security management	Data analysis	Data Governance
	Data management	Consent management	Risk assessment
CRM Roadmap	Agile project management	Measuring ROI	Centre of Excellence
		Business analysis	
User Management	Training tasks	Salesforce champions	Change management
	User support desk	Measuring user adoption	AI functionality for users

At the end of this chapter, you should have a clear understanding of and strategy for the Salesforce Administrator function and role, so that they/you know exactly what to do on a regular basis to proactively maintain a clean, healthy and secure system.

Download this Salesforce Administrator Action Plan from the Resources page on our website.

SCAN ME

STARTING A NEW ADMINISTRATOR JOB

Within this chapter we get down to the basics of starting a new Salesforce Administrator role.

It can be tempting to jump straight into the technical fixes but before you do, you need to understand the business, their processes and their system.

You might be adopting a system that is not well used or loved, or in better circumstances, a great platform with good adoption upon which you can build. The first four weeks are likely going to be all about discovery, so below is a road map of how you might tackle your new role.

If you don't have a plan, you can feel overwhelmed, like an imposter and pulled from one thing to another without any strategic direction. Without any structure, you are going to start off on the wrong foot and it can landslide from there.

Instead, you need to step into your power, take the lead and execute a strategy, especially if you are a solo Salesforce Administrator.

If you are a solo administrator you will need to manage

upwards and downwards, communicating what needs to happen.

It might be the case that you are the solo Salesforce Administrator and people around you will not be able to advise you, which leaves all eyes on you. If you have a team around you, then you will play your part, but you will still need to have a broader understanding and knowledge of the business.

A solo Salesforce Administrator will wear different hats, from business analyst to Agile project manager, technical guru to change management consultant. You should always start with business analysis, then move to technical configuration and adoption to build a solution in the best way.

On our Supermums Consultancy Skills Course we teach the essential hat trick of business analysis, change management and Agile project management skills and provide a range of business analyst templates specifically tailored to Salesforce to equip our students for success. Find out more about the course on our book resources page.

So, let's talk strategy.

Below are three initial tasks to focus on. We will cover these in more detail within the rest of the book.

1. Start with business analysis.

- Talk to your manager and the CRM Executive Sponsor to understand the business strategy – what the business does, its three-year plan and key performance indicators.

- Learn about the different departments, teams, services, challenges, and priorities.
- Armed with this information you can prioritise future Salesforce requirements in an Agile project management approach.

2. Understand the CRM strategy.

- Why was Salesforce implemented, what were the measures of success for the CRM and how is it performing against the ambitions?
- What is the general culture and appetite towards the CRM?
- Who are the Salesforce champions and avoiders?
- Who engages in CRM Governance and the Centre of Excellence?

3. Undertake an org analysis on the current Salesforce Instance.

- A data review – how good is data quality and do people trust the data?
- A product review - which products are being used or integrated?
- A user review – what does good user adoption look like?

- A governance review – who is managing the updates to the system?
- A system review – how healthy and up to date is the system?

We are going to summarise some of these aspects in the Org Analysis Chapter. To make this easy for you, download our free Health Check template from our Book Resources page to guide you through these steps and document your findings.

SCAN ME

At the end of this chapter, you should feel confident about how to start a new job putting your best foot forward. To do the best job possible be confident and focused on what you need to know before diving into technical solutions.

PROFESSIONAL DEVELOPMENT

Within this chapter we explore the type of training you should pursue depending on your learning style and career path. It is worth also reading the chapter on career progression to help define your career ambitions.

Choosing a Salesforce training course to suit you depends on your learning style – for example, are you motivated to self-study? Do you prefer live training? Do you want to get hands on experience? Or access one to one guidance and support?

It is also worth evaluating if the training resource is credible in the eyes of potential employers and will give you a competitive advantage over others at interview. The most reputable and highest quality training courses for your CV are those led by Authorised Salesforce Training Providers.

There are both free and paid for training course options available:

- Learn with an Authorised Salesforce Training Provider like Supermums to get instructor-led training and be confident that it covers all the relevant, most up to date content.

- Learn with Trailhead – learn solo at your own pace with Trailhead, which is a free, self-study platform from Salesforce, where you complete the modules yourself and earn points and badges on your learning progression.
- Learn with other providers – there are a range of other independent providers also available that offer virtual and in person training.

How to Learn Salesforce

The first question to ask yourself is 'Do I know my preferred learning style and learning habits?'

If you find yourself struggling to learn something, or if you're not motivated to learn, then review the areas below and make sure you choose the right training provider to meet your needs.

There is no point choosing a free virtual on-demand training course if you can't motivate yourself, if you get overwhelmed by where to start or struggle to move forward without a structured timetable. You would be better off choosing a course that offers a structured timetable, live training, and a method for providing accountability.

There are four common learning styles:

- Visual – you enjoy seeing visual demonstrations of the product, run-throughs, watching videos, presentations, and pictures.

- Kinaesthetic – you enjoy practically working through exercises to get a feel. You enjoy learning by doing and getting stuck into the product to understand how it works.
- Auditory – you enjoy listening to people to understand how to do something, whether it's a live trainer, video, audios, podcasts etc.
- Auditory Digital – you prefer reading things to learn how to do something and need all of the detail to understand the rationale and logic behind things.

What Are your Learning Habits?

Live Training – are you motivated by having set times and dates with live trainers to take you through a learning journey to keep you accountable? Do you like working in groups and/or one-to-one with trainers and mentors to ask questions, seek advice and maintain concentration?

Pre-Recorded Content – are you self-motivated to plan your learning journey and complete learning modules to build your knowledge and confidence? Do you prefer working independently at your own pace to get study done in your timeframes and seek help from peers only if needed?

It's best to go for Quality Assurance!

It's best to select an Authorised Salesforce Training Provider such as Supermums as you can be assured the content is up to date, delivered live by certified instructors and is recognised for its quality content when you approach employers.

Choosing an Authorised Salesforce Training Provider will give employers confidence that you have been trained in all of the necessary content by certified instructors and help you stand out amongst other people at interview. It could also land you that higher salary as you have invested in good quality training.

Which Certifications?

To become a fully-fledged Salesforce Administrator, you want to go for the hat trick of administrator certificates – The Salesforce Administrator Certification, Advanced Admin Certification, and Platform App Builder Certification. These certifications will make you a confident administrator and give you the suite of skills to manage a system with 'clicks not code' on a daily basis.

The Admin Training and Certification will enable you to:

- Explain the Salesforce architecture and its key terminology.
- Build a Sandbox to create, test, and move data to a Salesforce production org.

- Compare different methods for granting users access to functionality and data.
- Customise applications to meet business requirements.
- Describe use cases for data management and validation tools.
- Analyse Key Performance Indicators (KPIs) with reports and dashboards.
- Automate business processes using key features and functionality.
- Use the Salesforce ecosystem and resources to implement and maintain your Salesforce org.

The Platform App Builder Training and Certification will enable you to:

- Set up business logic and process automation.
- Manage data modelling and management.
- Design user interfaces.
- Build and deploy new apps.
- Implement Salesforce fundamentals.

The Advanced Admin Certification will enable you to:

- Implement advanced Salesforce features.
- Set up security and access.
- Customise objects and applications.

- Audit and monitor the system.
- Set up process automation.

Developing your Product Knowledge

Beyond the admin certifications, all administrators will need to get familiar with Salesforce products as it's likely you will use at least one in your organisation. Depending on your professional background or expertise you can focus in on Sales Cloud, Service Cloud, Non-Profit Cloud or the range of Industries Clouds for example.

There is a difference between learning enough to pass an exam versus learning enough to really understand a product and knowing how to implement it. When you showcase a 'Product' certification on your CV, employers expect you to truly understand the product and to have the confidence to implement it. Successfully passing a product certification should represent the following skills:

- You can confidently conduct business analysis.
- You can ask the right questions.
- You can gather requirements.
- You can confidently implement the product for a team.
- You can confidently demo the product in an interview.
- You know how to advance the product with third party apps.

Certification Study Tips

We therefore recommend the following study tips to help you get equipped and knowledgeable with these certifications:

- Check out the Salesforce Exam Guide.
- Complete the Trailmix.
- Complete Supermum Instructor-Led and On-Demand Training Courses.
- Build a Demo of Relevant Functionality.
- Test out knowledge with Focus on Force Questions.

Learning Consultancy Skills

If you plan to take responsibility for gathering requirements, engaging stakeholders in digital transformation and managing a Salesforce implementation professionally, then you will need an additional skill set beyond the standard Salesforce certifications.

Skills that every Salesforce solo administrator or consultant should possess include:

- Agile project management
- Business analysis
- Change management
- DevOps

We recommend that you take our Consultancy Skills Benchmark Quiz to assess your baseline level of knowledge.

This can be found on the book resources page here.

SCAN ME

At the end of this chapter, you should have mapped out your timeline for completing certifications and decided on the best way to learn. Learning Salesforce is a marathon not a sprint so go at your own pace, schedule your learning and most importantly decide how you are going to celebrate when you land that shiny certification!

MANAGING THE SYSTEM

Within this section we explore the admin tasks needed to keep the system fit and healthy to ensure everything runs smoothly for users. You need to love solving problems every day in this role.

A critical outage of a system can bring a business to a halt, an error can disrupt sales or create customer dissatisfaction and lack of data visibility can hamper customer intelligence.

As a quick overview we are going to equip you with the skills, tools and templates to manage the system.

To get started it's important to do a wider technical audit to understand what technology is currently being used across the business. During a technical audit you will want to:

- Map out which Salesforce products or third-party apps

are being used.

- Evaluate which products are integrated with Salesforce and those that are not and identify where there may be issues with data silos and 360 view integrity.
- Confirm which products are business critical and assess how well the products are being adopted by the team.
- Check the products are up-to-date and that new product releases are being reviewed and implemented as needed.
- Assess document and image storage and archiving needs and solutions and if they are being synced and stored securely.
- Review documentation of the org and what has been built and why.

Within the following chapters we do a deep dive into:

- Org Analysis – How to undertake a health check on your org.
- Harnessing AI as an administrator – how to improve your efficiency using AI.
- Documenting your Org – how to document and manage your changes.
- Introducing DevOps – how to start using DevOps to manage system updates.
- Document Management – how to manage document storage in your org.

- Integration Management – how to manage data flow between systems.

Here is a quick summary of the to do list.

Weekly/Daily	Monthly	Quarterly
Error Logs	Document Management	Org Analysis
AI Features	Documenting your Org	Technical Audit
DevOps	Integration Management	Product Release Management

ORG ANALYSIS

Within this chapter, you'll find out how to carry out org analysis and run a health check. We also provide a downloadable template and some recommendations for free org analysis products.

As the Salesforce ecosystem has matured, so has each customer's use of the platform, adding complexity, new functionality and challenges. This means that, as an administrator, chances are you'll be tasked with digging into existing orgs more often than setting up new implementations.

If you find yourself inheriting an existing Salesforce system, there will always be an initial fear about what you will find when you look under the bonnet. For example, did you know that, on average, each Salesforce org has over 24,000 metadata items to manage. That means if you click on each setup item and review it for five seconds, it will take you more than four days to review everything in the org.[1]

In the overall appraisal of an existing org and review of legacy issues, it is important to go through a business analysis

---

[1] Hubbl Benchmark Report 2023, www.hubbl.com/campaign/benchmark-report-2023, accessed August 2023

cycle and understand their current business needs. This will enable an assessment of how well the system is performing functionally and technically against their needs. This can be achieved through a series of audits. we call this process a health check.

On our Supermums Consultancy Skills course we deliver a session on how to conduct a health check on an existing Salesforce org and share a free health check template. You can download the template from the book resources page.

How to Conduct a Health Check on Your Salesforce Org

Complete an Initial Business Analysis (BA) Consultation

Initially, you want to understand the original objectives and motivations for implementing the CRM. You will also need to establish what progress has been made towards these goals and the perceived challenges and successes to date. This will enable you to establish priorities for the health check and review.

To achieve this, you will need to conduct a BA exercise with the executive sponsor and with different departments to understand their services, current business priorities, drivers and motivations for using the CRM.

Product and User Adoption Review

Once you've completed the BA, the next stage is to carry out a technical audit of the system, particularly relating to user adoption. You first need to ask and understand the criteria for good user adoption and then implement checks and balances by installing a user adoption dashboard, if there isn't already one set up.

Then you'll need to assess which Salesforce products people are using with a detailed review of which features they are using for each product. This helps you to assess if they are making the most of the product features, whether they are aware of them all and whether they could glean more value from adopting more features.

Since Salesforce metadata is well structured, we recommend taking advantage of automated audit tools like Hubbl Diagnostics to help simplify current state diagnosis. For example, look for tools that help you review the utilisation of each object, organised by Salesforce Cloud. This will help you to complete the product and feature review section of the health check template linked to above. Automatically identifying native capabilities that users are not currently leveraging will enable you to be more efficient with your time and drive more value for your users.

Governance and Management Review

It's useful to reflect on whether you have a good governance framework in place. For example, do they have a Centre of

Excellence? A Salesforce champion group? A Salesforce technical team? Who is responsible for delivering on the four roles of a Salesforce Administrator to manage the system?

- System Appraisal – as part of the system appraisal, you will want to mobilise several reports, including the Salesforce optimiser report, security health check report, NPSP health check report and error handling. You'll also want to automate the Well-Architected review of your org. This can help uncover issues and recommendations for remediation. Salesforce recently released the Well-Architected framework to help drive customers to build more trusted, easy-to-use and adaptable solutions. We highly recommend you familiarise yourself with this content. **System Release Updates and Functionality Changes** that are scheduled by Salesforce for all systems may require updates, sandbox checks and release cycles. Such updates would include things like **Lightning Transition** and **Flow Transitions** as system architecture and functionality improves and evolves.
- **Other Software Releases** are introduced by Salesforce three times a year to innovate and evolve the system. These need to be appraised to assess their value to your Salesforce System.
- **The Salesforce Optimizer Health Check** – can be

used to improve features, clean up customisations, and reduce complexity. It is valuable to check how well your system is performing on a quarterly basis. You can run the Optimizer Health Check and review any suggestions that Salesforce flags as a potential issue. The Health Check might create a nice little backlog of **Optimizer improvements** that need doing that you can assess and prioritise as needed.

- **Field Audit** – in line with your data management plan, it can be useful to assess field adoption on a quarterly or bi-annual basis.
- **Error Logs** – it's recommended that a user license is purchased for Salesforce Administrator tasks and integrations that is an agnostic user and not related to an individual, so if this person leaves the organisation, a personal user account doesn't need to be deactivated and everything re-assigned. Error logs for Apex, NPSP and duplicates can then be allocated to this user profile and can be monitored accordingly and ideally would go to a group email address so multiple Salesforce Administrators can oversee the system subject to working patterns and holidays.

Data Governance and Management Review

At this step of the health check, you need to understand what data is valuable to the organisation to meet its business objectives. For example, how does the organisation use data to drive decisions, market activities and serve customers? Once you know which data fields are important, you can then conduct an audit on the quality of data within these fields.

I would also recommend you install a data quality app from the AppExchange and a complementary management tool. Once you have reviewed the quality of data, you can then improve the management of data integrity in the future and create a plan for cleansing any data as needed.

Hubbl Diagnostics is a free solution that provides a comprehensive overview into any Salesforce org. It aligns to the Well-Architected framework while providing executive-level visualisations to walk through the state of their org. With this free diagnostics tool, you can get a quantitative, objective understanding of where the org stands compared to the wider ecosystem, while gleaning machine learning-derived insights about what to do next.

The free app can be downloaded from the book resources page:

SCAN ME

At the end of this chapter, you should be fully equipped with various tools and templates you can use to carry out an org analysis and health check. This will enable you to understand the current situation of the Salesforce org and to prioritise and plan a list of deliverables to be executed.

Thank you to Hubbl Diagnostics for sponsoring this chapter. Hubbl Diagnostics are on a mission to uplift and empower the Salesforce ecosystem through powerful org intelligence. Their solution provides admins, architects and consultants with broad and actionable insights into any Salesforce org. Their proprietary metadata aggregation also provides benchmark data to easily measure and compare org complexity against others in your industry. Find out more about Hubbl on our Book Resources page.

HARNESSING AI AS AN ADMINISTRATOR

Within this chapter we explore how AI skills and knowledge can support a Salesforce Administrator's daily tasks to improve their efficiency and effectiveness in their role.

AI tools and skills are becoming essential for admins to handle their daily tasks more effectively. Here's how AI knowledge can support a Salesforce Administrator:

Automating Routine Tasks

Salesforce Administrators are often overwhelmed by repetitive, routine tasks such as data entry, record updates, and managing workflows. These tasks, while necessary, can consume a significant portion of the day. AI tools, such as those offered through Salesforce Einstein, can automate these activities, allowing admins to focus on more strategic work.

Example:

AI can be used to automatically cleanse and delete duplicate data. Instead of manually identifying duplicate records—a time-consuming and error-prone process—AI can quickly scan and merge duplicates, ensuring that the CRM system remains accurate and up to date.

Predictive Analytics for Informed Decision-Making

One of the most powerful applications of AI is in predictive analytics. By analysing historical data, AI tools can forecast future trends and outcomes, providing Salesforce Administrators with actionable insights that inform decision-making processes.

Example:

With predictive analytics, a Salesforce Administrator can anticipate customer behaviour, such as the likelihood of a lead converting into a sale or the probability of customer churn. This allows the admin to prioritise tasks and allocate resources more effectively, enhancing overall business performance.

Enhanced User Support with AI-Powered Tools

Salesforce Administrators are often the first line of support for users encountering issues with the platform. AI-powered tools, like ChatGPT, can significantly enhance this support by providing quick, accurate responses to common queries, thereby reducing the admin's workload.

Example:

ChatGPT can be integrated as a chatbot within Salesforce, handling routine inquiries such as password resets, how-to questions, and basic troubleshooting. This ensures users get the help they need quickly, while the admin can focus on more complex issues that require deeper expertise.

Optimising Workflows

AI can also assist in optimising workflows within Salesforce. By analysing current processes, AI tools can suggest improvements that streamline operations, reduce bottlenecks, and enhance efficiency.

Example:

An AI-driven analysis of a sales workflow might reveal that certain steps are redundant or that tasks could be better prioritised. The Salesforce Administrator can then adjust the workflow accordingly, resulting in faster turnaround times and a more efficient process.

Data Security and Compliance

Maintaining data security and compliance is a critical responsibility for Salesforce Administrators. AI tools can help monitor data usage and access patterns, flagging any unusual activity that could indicate a security breach. Additionally, AI can assist in ensuring the CRM system remains compliant with relevant regulations by automating regular checks and audits.

Example:
An AI tool could automatically monitor user activities within Salesforce, identifying any actions that deviate from normal behaviour, such as large data exports or unauthorised access attempts. This proactive approach to security helps prevent data breaches before they occur.

Continuous Learning and Skill Development

AI is not only a tool for automation and analysis but also a resource for continuous learning. By staying up to date with the latest AI developments, Salesforce Administrators can enhance their skill set and stay ahead of the curve in their field.

Let's talk about ChatGPT and why you should learn how to use it effectively.

OpenAI made a big splash at the end of 2022 with the rollout of the fastest growing app of all time - ChatGPT. Why was this such an important moment in time? Prior to this, using a Large Language Model (LLM) was only being tested by companies like OpenAI, the LLM owners, and a few adventurous companies.

ChatGPT was designed to be used by everyone and was the first widely adopted consumer facing LLM chatbot. It wasn't created specifically for Salesforce professionals or any specific professionals for that matter. It's backed by the power of the finely tuned GPT4 language model which is trained on most topics you can imagine.

ChatGPT was trained on Salesforce specific concepts, so it has information specific to your needs. Because it's a generative AI, it can be used to create solutions to problems it wasn't specifically trained to solve! This combination along with the flexible use cases creates an incredibly powerful tool to help you tackle your work smarter.

So, what exactly can you do with ChatGPT? Here is a list of some common use cases:

- Problem solving
- Writing training documents
- Validation rules and formula fields
- Summarising key topics for large texts
- Providing general knowledge on Salesforce topics
- Salesforce setup support
- Writing triggers and Apex code
- Creating flow diagrams
- Copy for email templates

Harvard Business School completed a study and determined that '*professionals who use ChatGPT are able to complete 12% more tasks, 25% quicker, and with 40% higher quality than those who are not using ChatGPT.*'

The first step is to just get in there and start practicing. Ask some questions, have some conversations, and see if you can practice asking questions in different ways to get the things you are looking for from ChatGPT.

The great thing about taking a deep dive to learn how to truly use ChatGPT is the knowledge transfers over to the Salesforce Einstein 1 Platform. Salesforce professionals now have to use the Einstein Copilot Studio to manage the use of AI inside the platform, and knowing how the AI responds to prompts is your key to success when using the studio. Copilot is setup much like ChatGPT and infused with the data in your org. The skills you gain when learning ChatGPT set you up for future success with Salesforce.

By the end of this chapter, you should have a greater understanding of how AI is rapidly transforming the role of the Salesforce Administrator, turning routine tasks into automated processes and providing deeper insights through predictive analytics. By embracing AI skills and knowledge, Salesforce Administrators can not only streamline their day-to-day tasks but also enhance their strategic value to the organisation. Continuous learning and the integration of AI tools are key to staying relevant in this evolving landscape. For those looking to deepen their AI skills and knowledge, resources like the Supermums AI Training offer valuable opportunities to upskill and stay ahead in the Salesforce ecosystem. Find out more about the training on our resources page.

SCAN ME

DOCUMENTING YOUR ORG

Within this chapter we look at quick and efficient ways of documenting your org using AI tools. As an administrator, you don't have time to spend manually documenting everything in Salesforce and all too often, this gets stuck in your backlog. Accurate Salesforce documentation is crucial to the way in which you do your job as your company scales.

We know how important Salesforce documentation is, but we also know how important it is to automate that work. Not only will automating this task help save time, but it will also ensure consistency for the team which will help ensure accuracy. In addition to lessening the backlog, here's why every Salesforce Administrator needs to use an AI-powered documentation tool like Sweep:

Troubleshoot Salesforce Faster than Ever Before

Troubleshooting Salesforce is a part of every job. But with Sweep's AI tools and visual interface, you'll be able to quickly trace configurations, automation rules, and custom fields back to their purpose. Plus, you can map out dependencies between different elements. This is crucial because changes to one element might impact others. With a couple of clicks, you can visualise how this change might impact other parts of the configuration, such as reports that rely on that field, and avoid negative consequences.

Expedite Salesforce Knowledge Transfer

Whether you're growing your team, having a team member change team, or losing a team member, Salesforce knowledge transfer is vital to maintaining the seamless functionality of your CRM. With AI-powered documentation, you'll have confidence in ensuring that new and existing team members can access the same, full, up-to-date information every time. Plus, new hires can use the documentation as a self-service resource as part of their onboarding instead of bothering other employees with specific questions about functionality.

Improve Salesforce Management Efficiency

Too often, Salesforce Administrators get stuck feeling like they are simply working at a 'Help Desk' rather than actively contributing to the growth of the company. Well-intentioned co-workers will make requests, sometimes redundant ones, and administrators will have to answer each one separately. With the proper documentation, these teammates will be able to find answers on their own. This ultimately helps free up the admin to tackle more strategic tasks.

Quickly Streamline Your Data Collection:

Streamlining your data collection can help improve the functionality of Salesforce but manually searching for rarely used fields or ones with inconsistent data can take time. With AI, you'll be able to immediately identify the fields that are unused or are being filled with the incorrect data so you can eliminate these quickly and efficiently.

Visualise the Entire Salesforce Environment

While Salesforce is an incredibly customisable and comprehensive platform, it is not known for being easy to understand. When using Sweep, you'll be able to immediately turn your business processes into visualisations, your non-technical go-to-market stakeholders will be able to see how different steps interact and identify potential bottlenecks or errors. This also makes it easier to align the business systems teams and the go-to-market teams.

Plus, Sweep's visual workspace gives you the power to be more proactive. Instead of reacting to requests or spending time fighting fires. You'll then be able to use that bandwidth to think strategically about how Salesforce can support business goals and processes. The accessible shared view of the configuration also gives you the opportunity to build a roadmap that reflects the wants and needs of your cross-functional stakeholders so you can ensure that everyone stays on the same page.

Ready to start using Sweep's AI-powered documentation?

Now you can: for free. It's time to change the way you Salesforce. Download the free Sweep AI tool from our Resources Page

SCAN ME

By the end of this chapter, you should have a greater understanding of how to document your org using Sweep and harnessing the benefits of AI. By embracing AI skills and knowledge, Salesforce Administrators can save time and share valuable documentation with the whole organisation. Continuous learning and the integration of AI tools are key to staying relevant in this evolving landscape. For those looking to deepen their AI skills and knowledge, resources like the Supermums AI training offer valuable opportunities to upskill and stay ahead in the Salesforce ecosystem. Learn more about tools and training via our Resources page.

Thank you to Sweep for sponsoring this chapter. Sweep is an AI-powered visual workspace for Salesforce. With Sweep, teams can build custom Salesforce functionality—such as smart automation, Slack alerts, dashboards, and more—in a fraction of the time without compromising the development quality. Sweep was built for teams tired of the Salesforce status quo. Their users are embracing a future that harnesses the power of AI, real-time data, and custom metadata to improve efficiency and efficacy. And that future starts with Sweep. Find out more about Sweep via our Book Resources page.

DOCUMENT MANAGEMENT IN SALESFORCE

Within this chapter we investigate the implications and solutions related to handling large volumes of documents in Salesforce with a view to significantly reducing costs, managing version history and co-ordinating visibility between different teams.

By adopting effective document management strategies and leveraging AI-driven tools, Salesforce Administrators can significantly improve compliance, boost their productivity and support their teams more effectively.

Streamlining Document Management

Salesforce Administrators are frequently tasked with managing a wide array of documents, such as contracts, proposals, and customer records. These documents are essential, but they can also create bottlenecks if not managed efficiently. Traditionally, documents might be stored across various platforms, leading to issues like version control errors, data silos, and accessibility challenges. Centralising document storage and management is a key step towards overcoming these issues.

Centralised Storage and Access: A central repository for all documents ensures that team members can easily access the most current versions of files. This reduces the likelihood of errors and inconsistencies, which can be particularly problematic when dealing with contracts and legal documents.

Version Control: Maintaining control over document versions is crucial. By implementing a system where all changes are tracked and managed, teams can avoid working on outdated files, ensuring consistency and accuracy across the board.

Secure Sharing: The lifecycle of documents rarely starts and ends in Salesforce. Documents often need to be shared across different teams, both within and outside the organisation. Ensuring this sharing is done securely, with appropriate permissions, helps protect sensitive information and maintain compliance with data protection regulations.

Enhancing Collaboration Across Teams

Effective collaboration is vital in sales operations, where multiple teams often need to work together on documents like proposals, presentations, and contracts. Integrating content management with the tools that teams already use can greatly enhance collaboration.

Real-Time Collaboration: Allowing multiple team members to work on documents simultaneously, with changes updated in real-time, can significantly speed up the review and approval process. This reduces delays and helps keep projects on track.

Embedded Workflows: Streamlining workflows by embedding them directly within the systems that teams use can reduce the need to switch between applications. This integration allows for smoother processes, such as document approvals and feedback loops, directly within the CRM platform.

Task Automation: Automating routine tasks, like document approvals and notifications, can free up time for Salesforce Administrators to focus on more strategic initiatives. This also helps ensure tasks are completed consistently and on time.

Leveraging AI for Smarter Document Management

AI offers powerful tools for enhancing content management, making it easier for Salesforce Administrators to handle large volumes of data and documents efficiently.

Content Analysis: AI can automatically analyse documents and extract key information, such as contract dates, parties involved, and key terms. This makes it easier to categorise, search, and manage documents, saving time and reducing the risk of human error.

Enhanced Search Capabilities: Traditional search functions often rely on file names or manually entered tags. AI-powered search can delve deeper, finding relevant documents based on content and context, which can be particularly useful when dealing with large datasets or complex queries.

Automated Workflows: AI can also be used to automate more complex workflows, such as flagging documents that may present compliance risks or need immediate attention. This helps Salesforce Administrators stay on top of critical tasks and ensures that nothing falls through the cracks.

Maintaining Compliance and Security

For Salesforce Administrators, ensuring that all data and documents are managed in compliance with industry regulations is a top priority. Implementing strong data governance practices and utilising tools that support these practices is essential.

Data Governance: Proper data governance involves setting and enforcing policies around data retention, access, and disposal. This ensures documents are managed in line with regulatory requirements, which is crucial in industries with strict compliance standards.

Encryption and Access Controls: Ensuring documents are encrypted both in transit and at rest, and that access is tightly controlled, helps protect sensitive information from unauthorised access and breaches.

Audit Trails: Keeping detailed records of who accessed which documents and when can provide valuable transparency and accountability. This can be especially important in the event of an audit or security review.

Box.com is one tool that encapsulates these capabilities, offering a robust document management system with powerful AI features designed to support Salesforce Administrators in their daily tasks. By integrating seamlessly with Salesforce and providing advanced security, collaboration, and automation features, Box can help Salesforce Administrators manage their content more efficiently and effectively, ultimately boosting productivity and ensuring smooth operations. Find out more about their product on our Book Resources page.

SCAN ME

By the end of this chapter, you should have a better understanding of how to successfully centralise document storage, improve collaboration, leverage AI for smarter workflows, and ensure compliance.

Thank you to Box for sponsoring this chapter. Box is the Intelligent Content Cloud, a single platform that enables organisations to fuel collaboration, manage the entire content lifecycle, secure critical content, and transform workflows with enterprise AI. Founded in 2005, Box simplifies work for leading global organisations, including AstraZeneca, JLL, Morgan Stanley, and Nationwide. By integrating Box with Salesforce, users can easily store, organise, and share their files, documents, and other content without ever leaving the familiar Salesforce interface. Box supports all verticals including: FinServ, Healthcare, Government & more. Find out more about Box on our Book Resources Page.

SYSTEM INTEGRATION

Within this chapter we take a deep dive into integration to help Salesforce Administrators navigate the right solution for connecting different technology platforms. Thanks to our integration partners CONVAYR and EXAH, the following chapter provides some excellent insights into Systems Integration.

As a Salesforce Administrator, you are at the forefront of data management and process optimisation within your organisation. The integration of systems to share data can transform how your organisation works, from eliminating silos to enabling decision making and action. This guide breaks down some integration strategies and methods relevant to Salesforce Administrators, emphasising how you can perform complex data integration tasks independently, without the need for specialist technical skills.

What Is Integration and Why Does It Matter?

Integration, in general, refers to the process of connecting different systems or applications to share data. This ensures information flows seamlessly across platforms, reducing manual work, knowledge gaps and improving data quality. For example, integrating a CRM with an ERP might automate the transfer of customer order details, providing a unified view for sales and operations teams.

When it comes to Salesforce, integration plays a pivotal role in managing organisational data. By linking Salesforce with tools like ERPs, marketing platforms, or support systems, integration ensures all teams work from the same up-to-date information, reducing errors and duplication. It automates repetitive tasks such as syncing customer profiles or updating inventory, saving time and boosting productivity. For instance, syncing customer data from a marketing event to Salesforce ensures sales teams have visibility into campaign engagement, improving follow-up effectiveness.

Moreover, integration combines and contextualises data from multiple systems, providing actionable insights to prioritise leads or track revenue trends. Most importantly, it ensures the right data reaches the right people at the right time. This enhances responsiveness, empowers timely decision-making, and significantly improves customer experiences by enabling faster, more personalised service.

Understanding ETL, Reverse ETL, and ELT in Data Integration

When it comes to integrating Salesforce with other systems, you will likely come across the terms ETL, Reverse ETL, and ELT. As an administrator, these are the three core methods for moving data across systems, each offering different benefits depending on the use case. There are other, more technical approaches to integration requiring specialist skills and knowledge which are not covered here.

ETL (Extract, Transform, Load)

In an ETL process, data is first extracted from a source system, then transformed into a suitable format (such as cleaning or restructuring), and finally loaded into the target system, such as Salesforce. This process is commonly used when data needs to be cleaned or combined before being imported into Salesforce. It's ideal for situations where data quality and structure are paramount prior to storage in Salesforce.

Reverse ETL

Reverse ETL is essentially the opposite of the traditional ETL process. It involves extracting data from Salesforce or a data warehouse, transforming it as necessary, and then loading it into other operational systems or applications. For example, you might want to push CRM data back into marketing platforms, customer support systems, or analytics tools. Reverse ETL helps make Salesforce data actionable across your organisation's operational systems, enabling teams to use that data more effectively.

ELT (Extract, Load, Transform)

ELT flips the order of transformation. In this process, data is first extracted from the source system and loaded into the target system (like Salesforce or a data warehouse).

Transformation happens after the data is loaded, within the target system itself. ELT is particularly useful for large-scale data integrations because it reduces the time spent on data transformation up front and allows the target system to handle the processing. It's ideal for situations where real-time data processing or handling large data volumes is a priority.

Each of these processes plays a unique role in integrating Salesforce with other systems and ensuring that your organisation's data is structured, cleaned, and made actionable across different platforms. Depending on the type of data workflows and systems you're connecting, you might find that one approach is more suited to your needs than the others.

Integration Strategies for Connecting Systems and Data to Salesforce CRM

As a Salesforce Administrator, one of the most important tasks is selecting the right integration strategy to connect Salesforce to other systems and data sources. The integration approach you choose can significantly affect cost, implementation speed, and ongoing maintenance efforts. There are several strategies to consider, each with its own set of benefits and challenges. Below is an overview of the key integration options.

Custom Integrations

Custom integrations are built using code, and while generally offering the most flexibility, they can come with time and cost considerations. These solutions are tailored to meet specific business needs, allowing for complex workflows and precise control over how data flows between systems. Custom integrations are ideal for organisations with unique requirements that 'off-the-shelf' tools cannot address. Developing and maintaining these integrations requires skilled developers, making them costly and time-consuming. Additionally, as business needs change, custom solutions often require ongoing updates and troubleshooting, which can be resource intensive.

Pre-Built Applications

Another integration option is using pre-built applications that offer 'out-of-the-box' integration solutions with a set of specific functionalities for common systems and applications. You can often find these as managed packages on the AppExchange. These applications come with pre-configured templates, workflows, objects and reporting, which makes setup faster than custom integrations. They often support working with popular applications from inside Salesforce, however the level of customisation these tools offer with regard to data management is limited compared to other solutions.

Point-and-Click No-Code Integrations

No-code integration tools provide an intuitive, user-friendly alternative to custom integrations. These platforms allow Salesforce Administrators to connect Salesforce to external systems without writing code. No-code tools are fast to implement, enabling you to set up integrations and manage data jobs quickly. This speed is crucial for businesses that need quick deployment without waiting for custom projects.

The cost-effectiveness of no-code solutions is another key benefit. These tools are designed for non-technical users, meaning Salesforce Administrators can take full control of the integration process. This reduces dependency on IT teams, allowing admins to create, modify, and manage integrations independently.

Modern no-code tools are highly scalable, which means they can easily adapt as your business grows or your integration needs change. As new systems or processes are introduced, these tools can be quickly adjusted without the need for complex redevelopment. Maintenance is also much easier, as no-code platforms handle updates and ensure integrations continue to work smoothly.

While they may not provide the deep customisation of bespoke integrations, they can often work in tandem by allowing admins to adjust workflows and settings to suit specific requirements. This balance of ease of use and flexibility makes no-code tools a strong option for many use cases.

Summary

Integration connects systems allowing them to share data seamlessly, transforming Salesforce into a unified platform for businesses. For Salesforce Administrators, mastering strategies to move data in and out of Salesforce ensures the right data reaches the right people at the right time.

Modern tools with flexibility and scalability offer an efficient, cost-effective way to connect Salesforce with various data sources and targets. While custom solutions might be the right fit for certain use cases, having the right integration tools allows admins to automate data workflows and pipelines, perform a wide range of data related tasks and maintain a high standard of data quality, creating a connected, data-driven business with Salesforce at its core.

Integration products

What is CONVAYR?

CONVAYR is a powerful, affordable no-code data integration and ETL tool. CONVAYR has full schema support with transformation, error tracking, scheduling, logging, email control and more. Admins use CONVAYR to configure, automate and manage data workflows and tasks, data pipelines and system integrations.

Find out more on the Resources Page.

What is Salesforce Data Cloud?

Salesforce Data Cloud, formerly known as Salesforce Customer 360 Truth, is a comprehensive data management platform that allows businesses to integrate, unify, and manage customer data across all touch points. It provides a single source of truth for customer information, enabling organisations to deliver personalised experiences, improve operational efficiency, and make data driven decisions.

Which Salesforce Integration Product to Use

Data Cloud is your Data Management Ally

So, what exactly is Data Cloud? Think of it as a super-organised library that connects all your digital data together in one location, making it easier to understand and use.

Key Features:

Combining Data from different sources: Whether it's customer info, sales data, transactional data or website analytics, Data Cloud brings it all together.

Real-Time Insights: Get near real-time information to make timely decisions.

Scalability: As your data grows, Data Cloud grows with you without missing a beat.

Real-World Example:

Imagine a school using Data Cloud to monitor student performance. Teachers can see near real-time updates on grades, attendance, and even extracurricular activities, allowing them to provide support where it's needed most.

What is MuleSoft?

MuleSoft is a comprehensive integration platform that simplifies the process of connecting disparate systems and applications within an organisation. Founded in 2006 and later acquired by Salesforce in 2018, MuleSoft offers a robust Anypoint Platform™ that provides tools for designing, building, and managing APIs (Application Programming Interfaces) and integrations. The platform leverages a flexible architecture that allows businesses to connect on-premises systems, cloud applications, and even IoT devices.

At the core of MuleSoft's offering is its ability to enable API-led connectivity, a modern approach to integration that involves creating reusable APIs to unlock data and capabilities from various systems. This not only accelerates the integration process but also ensures scalability and agility, essential for businesses looking to innovate rapidly.

How To Use MuleSoft

MuleSoft Makes Integration a Breeze

If Data Cloud organises your data pantry, MuleSoft connects all your kitchen appliances, ingredients and recipes so they work together.

Key Features:

APIs (Application Programming Interfaces): Think of these as bridges that let different software applications share information.

Automation: Reduces manual tasks by automating workflows between systems.

Integration of multiple tools: Connects various tools, whether they're on-site or in the cloud.

Real-World Example:

Consider an educational platform that needs to:

Process payments

Update student records

Provide access to learning apps

MuleSoft ensures all these systems are connected, so when a student enrols and pays, they automatically gain access to the courses and resources they need. Data Cloud would house this information in its 'Data Lakehouse', but MuleSoft consolidates and transfers information from different sources of data for much larger use cases as well.

Thank you to CONVAYR and EXAH for sponsoring this chapter.

CONVAYR is a powerful, affordable no-code data integration & ETL tool. CONVAYR has full schema support with transformation, error tracking, scheduling, logging, email control and more. Admins use CONVAYR to configure, automate and manage data workflows and tasks, data pipelines and system integrations.

EXAH is a leading provider of integrated technology solutions, serving enterprises and forward-thinking business leaders across Africa, the Middle East, and Europe. Specialising in Salesforce and Mulesoft, as well as marketing automation, blueprinting and related services, EXAH caters to industries such as FinTech, Healthcare, Consumer Goods, Commerce, Manufacturing, and beyond.

Its excellence in the field has been consistently recognised by Salesforce, awarding EXAH the title of Overall Implementation Partner of the Year for Sub-Saharan Africa for three consecutive years (2021, 2022, and 2023).

INTRODUCTION TO DEVOPS

Within this chapter we explore the world of Salesforce DevOps. DevOps, a combination of development (Dev) and operations (Ops) is the industry gold standard for how companies manage their Salesforce processes. It's an Agile way of working that empowers all Salesforce professionals to contribute to the development and release cycle, whatever their technical skills or role.

Among its core objectives, DevOps aims to:

- Improve collaboration between admins, developers and business stakeholders.
- Speed up deployments and testing along an automated release pipeline.
- Enhance the quality and reliability of new features and functionality.
- Increase the frequency of releases to production.
- Build resilience with full visibility into changes, including options for rollback and disaster recovery.

DevOps brings significant benefits to businesses, helping them get the most out of their Salesforce investment. More frequent releases, for example, mean teams can respond quickly and in a flexible way to changing business needs and opportunities. By continuously delivering small improvements and iteratively building out new functionality, teams are better able to respond to business priorities while incorporating continual feedback from stakeholders.

At the heart of this process, Git-based version control gives teams a powerful way to collaborate on and co-ordinate a complex pipeline with multiple contributors and different streams of development and customisation. Using a DevOps platform like Gearset, each contributor can interact with version control using 'clicks not code', pushing changes to release and keeping all teams' development environments in sync.

Version control also makes it possible to add automation to workflows, which dramatically reduces the huge amounts of time teams otherwise spend on manual and error-prone processes, such as deployments and testing. In turn, this frees up teams to spend more time adding value for their end users.

The Impact of Successful DevOps

As well as producing a whole host of business benefits, DevOps is critical for avoiding costly mistakes. When the principles of DevOps are applied, Salesforce teams not only minimise the risk to their orgs but also strengthen their ability to recover from faulty deployments. Here are two real-life examples:

- Introducing a breaking change. New changes can impact Salesforce functionality like online payment processes, meaning people can't donate or buy at a given point. This obviously has a hugely detrimental impact on sales income and the organisation as a whole. Robust testing through a DevOps workflow reduces the chance you'll deploy a bug to production, and version control means you can quickly revert a deployment if an issue does arise. Minimal downtime makes for a happy business and end users.
- Lost data that can't be recovered. Data loss is a nightmare scenario — but it's a reality that many teams face. You don't want to be in a situation where your deployment or data import is responsible for losing business-critical data.

  A mature DevOps process includes an incident detection strategy and a pre-planned recovery process, to ensure you have an easy way to restore lost data and metadata.

Who Is DevOps For?

DevOps expertise isn't just for the specialists. Precisely because DevOps is all about collaboration, the demand for talent is there at all levels. Whether you're seeking a new role as an admin, developer, architect or consultant, understanding core DevOps concepts, tools and workflows can get you a long way and help you to progress your career.

Opportunities for professionals with DevOps knowledge currently exist across all industries and types of company. Larger organisations and enterprises with bigger Salesforce teams and more complex processes are especially likely to need DevOps know-how and will pay a premium for that expertise.

DevOps has become the industry standard. As the Salesforce ecosystem realises the limitations and challenges of traditional org-to-org development methods, familiarity with DevOps tools is rapidly becoming essential. In fact, DevOps is now a job role in its own right, with companies hiring Salesforce DevOps specialists at an attractive salary band.

Given that DevOps can accelerate Salesforce development while also decreasing bugs and issues, it's no surprise that organisations are so willing to invest in DevOps tools and practices, to help retain their competitive edge.

How To Get DevOps Right

Learning about Salesforce DevOps is a gradual process and, as with any discipline, specialist expertise requires practical experience. As a broad outline, the following are the tools, concepts and processes you will become familiar with as you make progress on your DevOps journey.

As a beginner, you will:

- Learn about development on Salesforce and modern release management
- Practise deploying different metadata types between orgs
- Back up your data and metadata

As a novice, you will:

- Get to grips with the fundamentals of version control
- Start using a Git hosting provider, e.g., GitHub
- Practice committing metadata to version control

As a practitioner, you will:

- Build up a repository of Salesforce metadata
- Begin treating version control as the 'source of truth' for development
- Explore the benefits of different Git-branching strategies

As an expert, you will:

- Automate tests, monitoring and deployment steps in the release process
- Seed sandboxes with masked production data for more robust testing

- Learn about the tools available from Salesforce DX

As a luminary, you will:

- Ensure compliance with backups integrated into the release process
- Create a fast-flowing CI/CD pipeline you can visualise in one place

Advance your Career with Salesforce DevOps

The rapid adoption of Salesforce DevOps by companies across all industries and sizes is opening up exciting career opportunities for both new entrants and seasoned professionals in the Salesforce jobs market. Getting ahead of the game could be a smart career move, as adding DevOps knowledge and expertise to your Salesforce skill set will set you apart from the crowd and could put you on a lucrative path.

A great place to learn all about Salesforce DevOps is on the free training platform DevOps Launchpad. Here, you'll find industry-relevant courses and certifications for the Salesforce community, written by DevOps experts. Whether you're new to Salesforce, or have years of experience, there are resources that cover all aspects of DevOps, including certification tracks in Salesforce DevOps fundamentals and Salesforce DevOps leadership. The courses are broken down into bite-sized learning items with short quizzes to test your knowledge, enabling you to learn at your own pace and in your own time. You can download your certificates to add to your résumé and social profiles to demonstrate your skills.

DevOps Launchpad has been developed by Gearset, but the vast majority of the content is vendor-agnostic, designed to give you a solid understanding of core DevOps concepts and best practices. If you're a beginner, it will help you get up and running with DevOps, or if you've some experience it can help you improve your existing processes. Get your first DevOps Certification via Launchpad – Find the link in the Book Resources page on our website.

SCAN ME

By the end of this chapter, you should have a greater understanding of why DevOps is important and how to start your journey of applying DevOps solutions to manage changes in your org, plus benefit from free training to equip you with the DevOps skills to hit the ground running.

Thank you to Gearset for sponsoring this chapter. Gearset are the leading experts in DevOps and DevOps education with their DevOps Launchpad platform, which provides powerful solutions for metadata and CPQ deployments, CI/CD, automated testing, sandbox seeding and backups. It helps Salesforce teams apply DevOps best practices to their development and release process, so they can rapidly and securely deliver higher-quality projects. DevOps Launchpad is a free training platform for all areas of Salesforce DevOps, to upskill the Salesforce community through practical training and certification.

USER MANAGEMENT

Within this section we delve into the admin tasks needed to manage and support users in adopting the system. You are the change agent in this role, and we like to emphasise the three E's – your role is to engage, enthuse and empower your users.

If users are not sure how to use the system or they aren't bought into using it, then you might as well not have a CRM system in the first place.

Low adoption rates can lead to:

- Inaccurate Data: Without consistent data entry, the quality of data within Salesforce diminishes, leading to poor decision-making.
- Reduced ROI: Investments in Salesforce may not yield the expected returns if users do not take full advantage of its capabilities.

- Operational Inefficiencies: Workflows and processes become less streamlined when users are not fully utilising Salesforce features.

As a quick overview we are going to equip you with the skills, tools and templates to support user adoption.

To get started it's important to do an initial stakeholder mapping to understand who the users are, what is expected of them and what good user adoption looks like. During a stakeholder mapping you will want to:

- Map out the different users of the system and the products they will use.
- Evaluate how to measure good user adoption with clear KPIs.
- Confirm the culture of the organisation and best approach to change management.
- Assess the different stakeholder personalities and their feelings towards the CRM.
- Decide on the best approach to training and roll-out.
- Review the motivational strategies for encouraging good user adoption.

Within the following chapters we do a deep dive into:

- Change management – how to facilitate change within an organisation.
- Support desk – how to manage support requests from

users.

- Salesforce Champions – how to mobilise departmental champions.
- Training end users – how to establish a gold standard training strategy.
- Using AI for user adoption – how to harness AI to foster user adoption.
- Measuring user adoption – how to measure user adoption.

Here is a quick summary of the to do list.

Weekly/Daily	Monthly	Quarterly
Support Desk	Measuring User Adoption	Change Management
Training	Salesforce Champions	AI Functionality

CHANGE MANAGEMENT

Within this chapter, you will learn more about how to plan for change management in a professional way that enables you to enthuse, engage and empower stakeholders at all levels.

What is Change Management?

The four key principles of change management are:

1. Understanding the organisational need, culture and readiness – this will tell you what approach is most appropriate for the organisational culture and history.
2. Understanding different stakeholder personalities – this involves knowing who the different stakeholders are, as well as their different personalities and learning styles, identifying the enthusiasts and the blockers.
3. Empowering people to lead change – this means equipping the executive leader to lead change and creating short to long-term teams, for example a change management team, Salesforce champions and a Centre of Excellence.
4. Implementing a project communications strategy – this is about planning communications throughout the

project, explaining the why, what and when in at least three different ways to enthuse, engage and embed.

Why is Change Management Important for Adoption?

If change management principles are ignored, there is a probable chance that stakeholders won't be engaged, enthused, or empowered enough to engage with the Salesforce system, because:

- The business case is not clear or communicated.
- People are not clear on why the change is important and buy-in is low.
- People do not feel consulted and are frustrated or disengaged.
- This will lead to:
- Input into the design being limited.
- A poor technical solution.
- The project being delayed.
- User adoption being low/nil.

If you harness change management, you will boost adoption. At Supermums we teach four pillars of change management to maximise the success of your Salesforce project. These pillars are not linear but layered throughout the project life cycle; they are:

- Analyse
- Plan
- Strategy
- Change

Let's talk through each of these in detail.

Analyse: Understand the rationale and readiness for the Salesforce project.

This pillar leads us back to the importance of BA skills, as analysis is a core component of change management. Stakeholders need to understand why the CRM project is important. They need to know the business case and rationale for undertaking the project. It's also important to understand the correct timing for the project. A risk analysis needs to be undertaken to identify and understand the risks so that you can design and implement an effective risk mitigation strategy.

Plan: Decide on an approach and gather a change management team for the Salesforce project.

This pillar relies on your Agile project management skills, as you are co-ordinating a change management project plan to be delivered by a change management team. The CRM project management plan needs to dovetail with the change management project plan to ensure everything is aligned. The two are fundamentally different but need to be interwoven. The focus of a change management plan is on communication to engage stakeholders. This plan will be executed by a range of people, from senior managers to HR, internal marketing, operations and governance, all of whom will make up the change management team.

Strategy: Mobilise leadership to execute the plan and engage stakeholders for the Salesforce project.

Once the change management plan has been agreed, the executive sponsor and leadership team need to be mobilised by being given clear roles and responsibilities. The leaders will need to communicate to the business and teams what is happening, when and why. Management needs to be aware and bought into the strategy in advance to support the execution of the plan and communication campaigns. To enthuse, engage and empower stakeholders will require a mix of communication methods to respond to different motivational and learning styles.

Change: Prepare for the Salesforce roll-out and embed changes as the norm.

In anticipation of the roll-out it's important to prepare an adoption strategy with a set of processes in place to create a carrot and stick approach for adoption. Ideally, you want users to feel enthused, empowered and engaged in the process, but you will also need to look at ways to embed these changes as the norm through institutional and compliance changes. Once a system is rolled out, how do you embed a change management culture going forward and establish quality control to check that adoption is at the expected levels, and to evaluate success?

At the end of this chapter, you should have a better understanding of why change management is an essential ingredient in a transformation project, and how you can plan a strategic communication campaign to engage stakeholders throughout the project life cycle.

SETTING UP A SUPPORT DESK

In this chapter, we explore the importance of setting up a Salesforce Support Desk and provide best practices for managing user communication and support effectively.

Why Setting Up a Salesforce Support Desk is Essential

For Users it provides:

- Clear communication channels: Users need to know how to ask for help or clarification when using the system. Without this, frustration and disengagement can quickly arise.
- Centralised resources: A one-stop shop for questions, answers, and training resources is essential for efficient support.
- Transparency: Users benefit from visibility into the status of their requests, enabling them to track progress and outcomes.

For Salesforce Administrators it provides:

- Streamlined communication: A single point of contact for new requests helps avoid the chaos of managing inquiries from multiple sources.
- Prioritisation: A consolidated view of all cases ensures requests can be organised and addressed based on their urgency and importance.
- Efficiency: Providing self-help resources and training materials reduces the volume of basic inquiries, freeing up time for higher-value tasks.

How to Set Up a Salesforce Support Desk

We recommend creating a dedicated Support Desk App within Salesforce, easily accessible via quick links from other applications. This app should include:

- A Home Page Interface: A central hub that directs users to key resources.
- Self-Help FAQs: Leverage knowledge articles to provide instant answers to common questions.
- Training resources: Integrate an LMS system or a video library to support continuous learning or utilise In-App Guidance or third party in situ training apps.
- Case form: A streamlined interface for users to create new cases.
- Case management guidance: Clear instructions on how to log, categorise, and prioritise cases.

- Case tab: A view for users to track their existing cases and their status.
- Learning tab: A section where you can assign Trailhead modules or other learning paths to users.

Additional Features to Include in the Support Desk App:

- Multi-channel support: Ensure users can create cases via email, chat, or an embedded form on the company's website in addition to the Salesforce app.
- Automated case assignment: Use case assignment rules to automatically route cases to the appropriate team members based on predefined criteria.
- Case escalation rules: Set up escalation processes for high-priority or unresolved cases to ensure timely follow-up.
- Customer satisfaction surveys: Include a mechanism for users to provide feedback on the support they receive to help identify areas for improvement.

Advanced Tools and Integrations

- Integration with third-party tools: Incorporate tools like Slack or Microsoft Teams for notifications and collaborative case management.
- Chatbots: Use Salesforce Einstein Bots to address

common queries before escalating to human support.

- Analytics and reporting: Configure dashboards to track support desk performance metrics, such as average resolution time, case volume trends, and user satisfaction rates.

Best Practices for Managing Cases

Handling cases efficiently is a key responsibility for Salesforce Administrators. Without proper processes, managing a backlog can feel overwhelming.

To stay organised, adopt Agile project management principles. Refer to the Agile Project Management methodology detailed in a later chapter. This approach aligns case priorities with the overarching goals of the senior leadership team, providing a clear framework for decision-making.

Collect Comprehensive Case Information

When logging a case, gather the following details:

- Case type: Identify if it's a feature request, technical issue, training need, data integrity problem, process improvement, or something else.
- Description: Include detailed explanations and any relevant links or documentation.
- Related department/team: Specify which team or department the case impacts.

- Business impact: Assess the potential ROI or operational benefits.
- User impact: Determine if the issue is critical or a lower-priority improvement.
- Prioritisation and timeline: Define the urgency and expected timeframe for resolution.

Utilise Tools and Best Practices

To ensure effective case management:

- Log communications: Use case comments, email-to-case, or integrated communication tools like Slack to centralise discussions.
- Track time: Leverage time-tracking tools to monitor how long cases take to resolve.
- Maintain documentation: Attach all relevant files and documents to each case for a complete history.
- Measure ROI: Evaluate the outcomes of resolved cases to demonstrate the value of your work to the organisation.

User Adoption and Training

To ensure users know how to use the support desk, implement the following:

- Onboarding sessions: Provide training for users on how to interact with the support desk, submit cases, and access resources.

- Regular updates: Communicate updates to users about new features or changes to the support desk.
- Feedback mechanism: Establish a process for users to suggest improvements to the support desk.

If you are the sole Salesforce Administrator it's important to have in place a support contract with a Salesforce consulting partner so you can access additional expertise and support as needed to complete technical tasks beyond your capabilities or to access mentoring so you can learn new skills to solve a solution. This support contract should be accommodated with the budget allocated to Salesforce and is often cheaper than hiring experts in-house with more advanced skills. As an admin there will be things that are beyond your technical remit. If you are looking for a Salesforce support partner, check out CloudGaia below.

By the end of this chapter, you'll create an efficient and user-friendly Salesforce Support Desk that meets the needs of both users and administrators.

Salesforce, the world's leading customer relationship management platform. CloudGaia brings Salesforce to life for the needs of businesses looking for fast, measurable and high-impact results using Agile methodologies. It has more than 230 employees in different parts of the world. CloudGaia reinforces its commitment to communities, the environment and the future through its Pledge 1% commitment.

ESTABLISHING SALESFORCE CHAMPIONS

Within this chapter we look at the role of a Salesforce champion and how they support the wider Salesforce Administrator function.

A Salesforce champion is the representative of Salesforce within their team or department whilst also doing their existing job role.

Why Have Salesforce Champions?

A Salesforce champion becomes the go to person for issues, ideas, and solutions within their department. Champions can have delegated admin responsibilities so they can provide cover when the central Salesforce Administrators are on holiday or sick.

Roles and Responsibilities of a Champion

A champion can have different levels of responsibilities from facilitating meetings to becoming a delegated admin. The role can offer progression where they start doing a few things and then they get more responsibilities as they train up in Salesforce Administrator and business analyst skills.

Responsibilities can include:

- Facilitating team discussions to identify current challenges or improvements desired by Salesforce users with a view to trying to resolve them.
- Providing onboarding and training new team members on how to use Salesforce.
- Analysing user adoption and troubleshooting issues.
- Managing duplicates and data integrity.
- Undertaking business analysis workshops and mapping out processes with the team.
- Working with managers to produce a business case for new requirements.
- Making changes to the Salesforce system to meet users' needs.
- Updating training resources if the system is updated.

How to Select Salesforce Champions

It is recommended that you conduct an interview process for champions as you want to pick someone with the right skills, motivation and experience to take on the job.

It can be beneficial to promote incentives, such an increase in salary, promotion and training opportunities so they can see it as a career progression.

You would ideally want to advertise the opportunity amongst the team and then go through a shortlisting and interview process. Ultimately you are looking for:

Skills – if they have some Salesforce Administrator experience already then that's great, but alternatively you would be looking for someone that is good and quick at learning technology and enjoys improving businesses processes to produce better outcomes for the team and customer.

Personality – typically you are looking for a good listener, questioner, problem solver and fixer.

Experience – ideally, they would have had experience with Salesforce and CRMs before, but this isn't essential, just a nice to have. They would also have experience of training individuals.

Motivation – individuals are often motivated by reward, so the opportunity to upskill, earn more or get a promotion will appeal.

How to Upskill Champions

It depends on the roles and responsibilities you want a champion to have.

If you want them to understand Salesforce but not be an actual administrator, you could get them to complete the Salesforce Associate Certification with relevant trailheads to do.

If you want them to be a delegated Salesforce Administrator, then you would encourage them to complete the Salesforce Administrator certification. The training they undertake to do this should suit their learning style, so if they prefer live training, they might want to do the Supermums Authorised Salesforce Administrator course. If they are happy reading things, they may just want to do trails.

If you want them to produce business cases and conduct business analysis, then you might want to complete the Business Analysis Certification. They can complete the Supermums Consultancy Skills Course or learn business analysis in another way.

How to Manage Champions

Champions are part of the Governance Structure – As a representative for their team and department they need to collate issues and business priorities and present this back to the Salesforce team and CoE. They shouldn't be part of CoE meetings directly, but they should have regular meetings with the in-house Salesforce team to report back and discuss progress.

It's important to give them the opportunity to learn and discuss Salesforce learning, products, problems, and issues with their peers and to feel like a member of the team rather than working in isolation. It can be useful to arrange informal Salesforce lunches to bring your champions together to discuss certifications, new features, and tools. You could invite them to user group meet-ups.

There will be an element of performance management within this role as there are job responsibilities and so there needs to be a feedback loop with their direct line manager. There should be performance objectives, KPIs and learning opportunities all built into the role.

An internal Salesforce support desk can co-ordinate all the different cases amongst champions especially if they have a delegated admin role. They can respond and update cases that are relevant for their team and department.

A communication and file sharing platform is valuable to keep conversations and the lines of communication open to discuss any of the above factors in between meetings. When you all work in different departments it can be easy to get siloed. Having a mutual platform for communication and sharing files related to Salesforce work is imperative to teamwork.

At the end of this chapter, we hope you have the right information to identify suitable champions and put in place a framework to support their new roles that bridge the Salesforce team and users within their departments.

TRAINING END USERS

Within this chapter we'll look at a gold standard training strategy that will equip users with the skills to use the system and bolster adoption.

To refine and work towards a perfect training strategy, you need to take into consideration:

- Different learning styles
- Different motivations
- Different training mediums and approaches

The success of a Salesforce implementation often lies in supporting people to engage with the process and system, rather than the technical skills involved in building the system.

Learning Styles and Motivation

Learning styles can be understood using the VARK model. Under this model, there are four learning styles: visual, auditory, read/write, kinaesthetic. Can you identify your learning style? Quite often, we can be a combination, with a primary and secondary preference. Below is an example scenario that could help you work out your preferred learning style:

If you are putting together some DIY furniture, what do you

like to do?

- Watch a video (auditory)
- Read the manual/instructions (read/write)
- Follow the pictures (visual)
- Just have a go without consulting anything (kinaesthetic)

You can also take a learning style test, and you could use this with people you are training to uncover their styles too. This is particularly valuable for one-to-one mentoring. In a group setting, you want to appeal to all learning styles.

To get this right and tick all the above boxes, you'll need to think about how you are going to deliver the training content in a range of mediums. Below are some ideas:

- For read/write types, you need to prepare a training manual and Trailheads, as they prefer reading text.
- Visual types will prefer pictures, videos, live training sessions, slides.
- For auditory learners, you'll need live training, with verbal instruction and/or videos etc.
- For kinaesthetic learners, providing user scripts to run through will help them experience the content they're learning.

Access to Training Resources

Once you have delivered the training, you need to think about where the training resources are going to be kept so that people can continue to refer to them. You have a few options here. The basic method, and a quick and easy solution, is to set up a shared external folder in a digital filing system. You could also use folders or the knowledge articles in Salesforce, ideally with quick links embedded around the Salesforce system to navigate people back to the training resources.

Alternatively, you could introduce an LMS (learning management system). The benefit of an LMS is that you can upload content and set a training plan for your users in an ordered fashion. This will also provide an audit trail, showing you whether people have completed and watched the training material, meaning non-adopters can be flagged easily, and a motivational strategy utilised.

You could use native in-situ training resources, setting up training tools that are already embedded in the Salesforce system and easy to find – think Trailhead Paths, My Trailhead, Learning Paths and In-App Guidance. You could also consider third-party in situ training and adoption tools. These enable you to embed content, such as instructions and videos, around your Salesforce org to boost digital adoption within your user communities.

How to Evaluate Success

The success of a training strategy is indicated by the end-user adoption analytics. Are they as expected? Ask for feedback on the training and host a follow-up session for reflective learners in case they have any questions.

For further reading on Salesforce training, 'Improved Apps' have published some useful white papers on this subject. You can find these linked on the book resources page.

SCAN ME

'Improved Apps' white papers:

- Delivering zero classroom training
- Top ten tips for driving digital transformation, usage and adoption in the current climate
- Guide: How to get employee Salesforce onboarding right first time
- Guide: How to deliver Salesforce training that sticks
- Guide: 6 steps to successful just-in-time learning in Salesforce

At the end of this chapter, you should have a comprehensive understanding of how to create a holistic training strategy that can engage people with different learning styles and meets the needs of end users. You know how to prioritise training in your allocation of time and budget, and how to measure its success by looking at user analytics.

Thank you to Improved Apps, the only Salesforce security-reviewed digital adoption partner, for sponsoring this chapter. Improved Apps are passionate about educating Salesforce professionals about digital adoption and can help you embed your content in context to boost digital adoption within your user communities. Their free Improved Usage Tracker tool gives insights, data and dashboards to show you exactly how your users are engaging with Salesforce, enabling you to identify the potential for efficiencies and boost productivity for greater Salesforce ROI.

HARNESSING AI TO SUPPORT USER ADOPTION

Within this chapter we explore the role AI is playing in helping admins and users overcome the barriers to adoption. AI has the potential to transform the Salesforce user experience by automating tasks, providing personalised assistance, and enhancing data accuracy.

How AI Enhances Salesforce User Adoption

Here's how AI can address some of the common challenges associated with Salesforce user adoption:

Personalised Onboarding and Training

One of the primary reasons for low user adoption is inadequate training. Traditional training methods often fail to account for the varying levels of experience and learning styles among users. AI can revolutionise onboarding and training by offering personalised learning experiences tailored to each user's needs.

AI-driven platforms can assess a user's proficiency with Salesforce and customise training modules accordingly. For instance, a novice user might receive step-by-step tutorials and basic explanations, while a more experienced user could be offered advanced tips and shortcuts. This personalised approach ensures that each user receives the appropriate level of guidance, accelerating their comfort and proficiency with Salesforce.

Intelligent Data Entry Assistance

Data entry is a crucial but often tedious task for Salesforce users. Inconsistent or incomplete data entry can lead to inaccuracies, which undermine the effectiveness of the CRM system. AI can alleviate this burden by automating data entry and ensuring data consistency.

AI-powered tools can automatically populate fields based on context, predict the correct entries based on past behaviour, and prompt users to complete missing information. This reduces the manual effort required for data entry and minimises the risk of errors. As a result, users are more likely to engage with Salesforce regularly, knowing that the process is streamlined and supported by AI.

Smart Automation of Repetitive Tasks

One of Salesforce's strengths is its ability to automate workflows. But setting up these automations can be complex and time-consuming. AI can simplify this process by analysing user behaviour and suggesting automations that can save time and increase efficiency.

For example, AI could identify patterns in how a sales team manages leads and automatically create workflows that align with those patterns. This reduces the time users spend on repetitive tasks, allowing them to focus on higher-value activities. When users see that Salesforce can reduce their workload through AI-driven automation, their engagement with the platform is likely to increase.

Enhanced Predictive Analytics

Salesforce's reporting and analytics capabilities are powerful, but they require users to understand and interpret large amounts of data. AI can enhance these capabilities by providing predictive analytics that offer actionable insights without the need for extensive data analysis skills.

AI algorithms can analyse historical data within Salesforce to predict future trends, such as which leads are most likely to convert, or which accounts may churn. By presenting these insights in an easy-to-understand format, AI empowers users to make data-driven decisions quickly and confidently. This not only increases user adoption but also improves the overall effectiveness of the Salesforce platform.

AI-Driven Customer Interaction

Salesforce is widely used for managing customer interactions, but ensuring these interactions are consistent and effective can be challenging. AI can support users by providing real-time recommendations during customer interactions, such as suggesting the best response to a customer inquiry or identifying upsell opportunities.

For instance, an AI tool could analyse a customer's history and suggest personalised product recommendations during a sales call. This level of support enhances the quality of customer interactions and makes Salesforce an indispensable tool for users, thereby driving adoption.

Following this chapter, it is worth evaluating the areas of business need and appraising the AI tools available in the Salesforce eco-system to improve areas of efficiency and support your end users in their daily use of the system.

MEASURING USER ADOPTION

Within this chapter, find out how to create a user adoption strategy that will embed the Salesforce system for the long term beyond the initial training.

Firstly, when encouraging users to adopt the system, you can take a carrot or stick approach.

The Carrot Approach

The carrot approach is about providing positive incentives and motivations to adopt the system. Some ways of applying this strategy are to:

- Realise the benefits that individuals requested from the system and communicate these during training.
- Generate reason(s) to login into the system everyday – for example, to respond to new enquiries or cases that are no longer being routed by email.
- Utilise CRM team collaboration tools for stakeholder discussions.
- Introduce gamification. For example, if a deal is won, the system can send a celebration alert to the whole team or give prizes to people earning the most

Trailheads points.

- Create a reward system based on performance data that is captured within CRM reporting dashboards that are shown in team meetings.
- Celebrate success – identify the big wins and benefits of using the system and share these across the teams.

The Stick Approach

By contrast, the stick approach is less about incentives and more about setting an expectation, and/or suggesting negative consequences for not adopting the system. For example, you could:

- Create an official go-live date and time when everyone has to start using the system.
- Deliver continuous and targeted communication through a range of lean and rich communication methods and repeat these so all intended users see and hear messages about the system go-live at least three times – often, people don't acknowledge a message until the third time they see it.
- Set out and maintain clear business rules within the training manual for use of CRM. For example, expectations around when calls or emails need to be logged, which fields of data need to be completed, when contacts should be added into the system. This level of

detail is imperative when teaching someone how to use a CRM system.

- Rewrite job specifications and contracts to include requirements about when and how they need to use the CRM as part of their job. Then, if they don't input information into the CRM, or refuse to use it, you can go down a performance management route to ensure adoption.
- Utilise the CRM dashboards for performance management in team meetings and one-to-ones to showcase team performance. Champion the Salesforce Ohana mantra of, 'If it's not in Salesforce, it doesn't exist.'
- Align reviews or bonus payments to performance information captured within the CRM to keep people focused on what they need to do to achieve their goals.

Key Pillars for Embedding the System

There are five key pillars for embedding a Salesforce CRM system: having a support desk in place, institutionalising change as the norm, establishing a change culture within the organisation, establishing quality control and evaluating the success of the project.

Below are some of the actions you can take within each of these pillars.

Having a Support Desk in Place

- Look at ways to embed on-demand training resources within your system so it is easily accessible to users. You can use the tools that we mentioned in the previous chapter to embed training content that can give real-time support to users to navigate and use the system.
- Provide an ongoing support service to ensure the team has easy access to answers, advice or coaching as required.
- Set up a CRM support desk so users can raise cases for issues, training requests or any ideas they have.
- During the first six months after go-live, set up regular working groups with users to invite verbal feedback from people so that you unearth any hidden dramas that might be arising.
- Share learning and any updates with the team to embed a continual improvement process.
- Produce resources that can be shared and accessed as required by the team.

Institutionalising Change as the Norm

- Establish new expectations of managers, staff or stakeholders as the norm.

- Redesign job roles and partner contracts etc.
- Establish new KPIs and performance management frameworks.

Establishing a Change Culture in the Organisation

- Foster an environment of continual change to improve quality and maximise opportunities.
- Maintain a champions team and ongoing feedback loop from users to continue.
- Develop an evolution pathway for new and existing changes.
- Refine and embed the change management process for the future.

Establishing Quality Control

- Monitor whether the new approach is being adopted by the relevant teams and address any resistance as necessary.
- Maintain communication with users to solve issues, counter resistance or solve problems that are affecting use or outcome quality.
- Continue to refine and develop the solution based on feedback to ensure it meets requirements.

Evaluating the Success of the Project

- Evaluate the effectiveness of the change management process amongst different stakeholders.
- Collect and review feedback from users to see if the solution is meeting their expectations.
- Undertake a cost–benefit analysis to review whether the solution has produced the anticipated benefits.

How to Assess User Adoption

You can assess the level of adoption by identifying metrics that indicate improved productivity and engagement. But what to measure?

In light of tighter purchasing budgets, it is imperative to prove not only the ROI of technology purchases through usage but also increased productivity and engagement improvements through the use of Digital Adoption Solutions (DAS). To achieve this, application leaders/product owners must work to support the business units in creating a set of metrics that can be tracked.

Most often, these can also be correlated to money saved or improved revenue outcomes. Some examples of metrics you can use, ways of measuring them and outcomes they're linked to, are provided below.

1. Number of support tickets resolved, and time spent

resolving tickets.

Measurement:

- Number of 'how do I' tickets by application.
- Length of time taken to resolve issue.
- Outcome:
- Fewer tickets allow for more complex problem resolution and increased end-user satisfaction (higher engagement).
- Reduced length of resolve time allows 'N percent' group overall response time improvement.

Training Time Measurement:

- Reduced hours spent on onboarding and change management.
- Outcome:
- Decrease in training costs due to in-application learning.
- Artefacts created by DAS do not need to be created by the training department.
- Change management training may be eliminated.
- Training reinforcement leads to greater end-user satisfaction (higher productivity).

2. Onboarding time to productivity.

Measurement:

- Time from hire to fully productive
- Outcome:
- Reduced onboard time saves money and increases contribution rate for employee (e.g., less time to get a seller productive and delivering revenue).

3. Data quality issues.

Measurement:

- Data validation
- Outcome:
- Reduced data issues
- Increased data completeness

4. Employee satisfaction.

Measurement:

- Employee engagement survey scores, NPS score or similar satisfaction scores.
- Outcome:
- Increased satisfaction leads to higher engagement and productivity.
- Correlation to customer satisfaction.

There are some more useful white papers on this topic by 'Improved Apps', available on the book resources page.

- Guide: The three roadblocks to Salesforce adoption
- Guide: How to find out why people aren't using Salesforce

There is also a website (www.digitaladoption.info) offering a free learning platform for digital adoption and knowledge management, where you can access a plethora of information to aid in selecting the ideal digital adoption vendor for your business, ensuring you leave no stone unturned.

At the end of this chapter, you should have a clear idea on how to maximise and monitor user adoption with clear demonstratable results.

DATA AND SECURITY MANAGEMENT

Within this section we delve into the admin tasks needed to manage data and security to keep your system clean and safe. Your role is to be the data champion with a passion for clean trusted data. Think of yourself as the housekeeper.

The Salesforce Administrator team should work with the company's operational team to align the system to security and data protection policies. It's not a one-person job but a team effort to keep data secure, but the Salesforce Administrator team will be responsible for putting functionality in place to keep the CRM system as safe as possible. If there isn't a plan in place for keeping the system secure, then a data breach can occur.

A data breach is when people can access a system or see data they aren't meant to. If this happened, it would have to be reported to the Data Protection Regulators. It's important to test and ensure security access is set up and monitored as required. If there was a data breach, and it is likely that security policies within the system were not implemented correctly, the company could be subject to a financial penalty or damaged reputation.

As a quick overview we are going to equip you with the skills, tools and templates to manage data integrity and security.

To get started it's important to do an initial data and security review to understand what data is being collected, for what purpose and at what level of sensitivity. During this review you will want to:

- Review the risks and the data collected.
- Evaluate how to measure good data integrity and what the current quality is.
- Confirm which users should have access to which data.
- Assess how to monitor and manage data integrity going forward.
- Decide on the best approach to training and roll-out.

Within the following chapters we do a deep dive into:

- Security management – how set up and monitor the security of your system.

- Risk assessment – how to assess and mitigate potential risks.
- Data management vs governance – how is data being managed?
- Contact and consent management – how to manage contacts and consent.
- Data analytics – how to maximise the value of your data.

Here is a quick summary of the to do list.

Weekly/Daily	Monthly	Quarterly
Data Incident Review	Security Management	Risk Assessment
Contact and Consent	Data Analytics	Data Governance

SECURITY MANAGEMENT

Within this chapter we unpack the elements related to managing security in your system and how to craft a security policy that sets out your intentions and business rules.

To start building this picture, you will want to understand:

- Who are your users, how are they logging in, and how frequently? What data should they have access too? Are the user profiles set up correctly?
- What are the security requirements for different countries and regulations?
- What types of data classification does your system hold? For example, do you have highly sensitive fields and any that need to be encrypted?
- How should someone be logging in? Should they be using single-sign on and mydomain?
- What are the password policies for the organisation and how should this be managed in the system?

Once you understand the security requirements you can then implement, manage and oversee the security of the system and data.

Security Management

Once the security requirements have been implemented you can use various native and third-party apps to oversee and test the system. For example:

Security Health Check – As an admin, you can use Health Check to identify and fix potential vulnerabilities in your security settings, all from a single page. A summary score shows how your org measures against a security baseline, like the Salesforce Baseline Standard.

Security Centre App – The Security Centre app offers a single view of your security, privacy, and governance posture across all your Salesforce orgs and tenants. Use the app to review up-to-date health check scores, access settings, user and login metrics in one easy-to-read interface.

Salesforce Shield – Salesforce Shield is a trio of security tools that helps admins and developers build extra levels of trust, compliance, and governance right into business-critical apps. It includes Shield Platform Encryption, Event Monitoring, and Field Audit Trail.

Assessing risks is an ongoing task and it's important to have a Data Incident Response Plan in place to know what to do in the event of a data or security breach. Download further guidance and resources to build your Risk Assessment and Data Incident Response Plan from our Book Resources page.

SCAN ME

Thank you to CloudAlly for sponsoring this chapter. CloudAlly's SaaS Data Protection platform secures the data of all major SaaS platforms with fully automated cloud-to-cloud backups.

Comprehensive high-availability SaaS data protection of Salesforce, Microsoft 365, Exchange, SharePoint, OneDrive, Teams, Google Workspace, Dropbox, and Box.

DATA MANAGEMENT VS DATA GOVERNANCE

In this chapter we unpack the difference between data governance and data management and the role of a Salesforce Administrator in delivering on these two concepts working closely with the data protection officer.

When it comes to data handling, two key terms often conflated are data governance and data management. While they may sound similar, these critical concepts serve distinct purposes in the data landscape.

Below, we break down the nuances between the two to understand their roles and how they work in tandem:

What is Data Management?

Data management involves the organisation, storage, retrieval, and processing of data throughout its lifecycle. It encompasses tasks like data integration, storage optimisation, and data cleansing.

Data management focuses on operational efficiency and meeting the immediate needs of an organisation's data users.

What is Data Governance?

Data governance is the framework of policies, procedures, and standards that define how data should be managed, maintained, and used across an organisation. It involves establishing rules for data usage, designating ownership and accountability, and providing the structure necessary for effective data management.

Data governance ensures compliance with regulations and standards.

What's the Difference Between Data Governance and Data Management?

If you're still wondering, 'How is data governance different from data management?', the differences may become clearer once we break them down by scope, focus, and implementation.

Scope:

- Data management deals with the technical aspects of handling data, like storage and processing.
- Data governance addresses the broader aspects of data strategy, including policies, compliance, and risk management.

Focus:

- Data management focuses on the day-to-day operations of handling data efficiently.

- Data governance focuses on establishing rules and guidelines to govern data usage, ensuring its quality and reliability.

Implementation:

- Data management leverages tools and technologies to manage data more effectively.

- Data governance establishes policies and procedures to govern data usage and employs data stewardship to ensure compliance with regulations.

How Data Governance and Data Management Work Together?

Data governance and management are complementary processes that work hand in hand to ensure the effective use of data within an organisation. While data management handles the technical aspects of data handling, data governance provides the framework and guidelines to ensure appropriate and responsible use of data.

This creates a symbiotic relationship wherein data management deals with the 'how' of handling data, while data governance addresses the 'who', 'what', 'when', and 'why'.

Documenting Success with Data Governance

Implementing data governance is a significant investment for any organisation, and measuring its success is crucial for ensuring that it delivers tangible benefits and returns on that investment. Here are some key metrics and approaches for measuring the effectiveness of data governance initiatives:

Data quality metrics

One of the primary goals of data governance is to improve data quality. Measure metrics like data accuracy, completeness, consistency, and timeliness to assess the impact of data governance efforts on data quality improvements. Regular data quality assessments and audits can provide valuable insights into areas that need attention.

Compliance and risk management

Evaluate the organisation's compliance with regulatory requirements, industry standards, and internal data management and privacy policies. Measure the reduction in compliance risks, such as data breaches or regulatory fines, as a result of implementing data governance practices.

Data access and security

Assess data governance effectiveness by controlling and protecting sensitive data from unauthorised access or breaches. Monitor metrics such as user access controls, data encryption, and compliance with data security standards to ensure data security and privacy.

Data usage and consumption

Measure the usage and consumption of data assets across the organisation to gauge the effectiveness of data governance in enabling data-driven decision-making and business outcomes. Track metrics like data utilisation rates, user adoption of data governance tools and processes, and data governance impact on business performance.

Stakeholder satisfaction

Gather feedback from stakeholders, including business users, data owners, and IT professionals, to assess their satisfaction with data governance initiatives. Conduct surveys, interviews, or focus groups to understand stakeholders' perceptions of data governance effectiveness, usability of data governance tools, and alignment with business objectives.

Time and cost savings

Measure the time and cost savings achieved through streamlined data management processes, improved data quality, and reduced errors. Quantify the reduction in manual effort, data processing time, and operational costs resulting from data governance initiatives.

Data governance maturity

Evaluate the maturity level of data governance practices and capabilities within the organisation using frameworks such as the Data Management Maturity (DMM) model or the Capability Maturity Model Integration (CMMI). Track progress over time and identify areas for continuous improvement to advance the organisation's data governance maturity.

By monitoring these metrics and continuously assessing the effectiveness of data governance initiatives, you can demonstrate the value of data governance, identify areas for improvement, and optimise your data management processes to drive business success.

Useful Tools for Data Management

As mentioned, data management relies on various tools and techniques to streamline data handling. Each tool serves a specific purpose in managing different aspects of the data lifecycle. For example:

Data cleansing tools: Identify and correct errors in data to ensure accuracy and consistency.

Validity DemandTools is a secure data quality platform that enables organisations to clean and manage Salesforce data in less time, allowing everyone to do their jobs more effectively, efficiently, and profitably.

Data integration platforms: Streamline the process of

combining data from multiple sources and help integrate data from various sources into a unified format for analysis.

By the end of this chapter, you should understand that while data management focuses on the technical aspects of handling data, data governance provides the overarching guidelines for its effective use. These processes manage data efficiently and responsibly to drive informed decision-making and business success.

MANAGING CONTACTS AND CONSENT

Within this chapter we look at how to best manage contacts and associated consent within Salesforce to comply with data protection and supporting data integrity and security.

The contact object is the anchor object of the CRM and therefore, it will be used by multiple departments to manage and store stakeholder contact information. The Salesforce Administrator needs to ensure that different departments are aligned on how to use the contact object with the following considerations:

- Contact records hold core data and other fields are valuable and populated.
- Contact records are owned by someone and duplicates are managed.
- Contact records can be easily segmented for marketing and comms purposes.

There are five areas to explore as part of contact management:

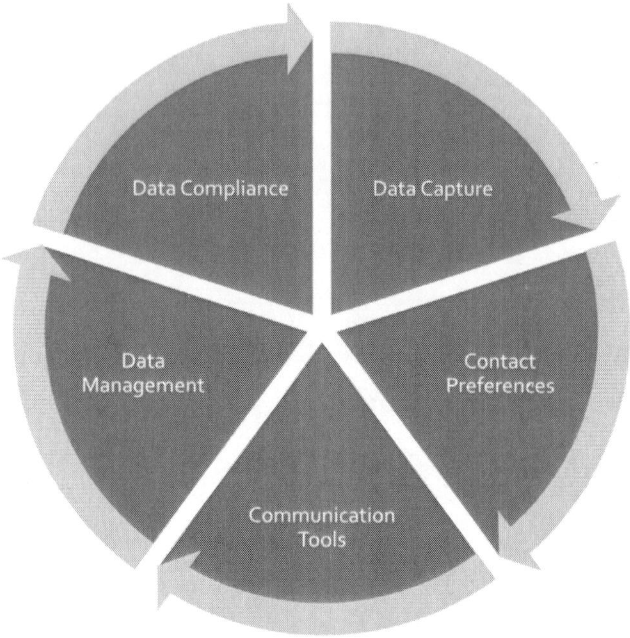

Data Capture

Firstly analyse how contact and consent information is being captured and then how it is integrated, imported or input directly into Salesforce. Secondly analyse what information you capture about a contact from compulsory data, core data, segmentation, categorisation to engagement with the brand.

Contact Preferences

Firstly analyse how contact data is used by different departments for their marketing needs, and how you need to segment your contacts for targeted communication e.g. by type of stakeholder or preferred contact method. Secondly appraise how stakeholders can manage their consent, opt in or out of communication preferences, and how people will be able to update their contact details, consent and interests over time.

Communication Tools

Firstly analyse the frequency and volume of the communications with different stakeholders and secondly what communication tools the team are going to need to communicate with them to meet their communication preferences.

Data Management

Firstly analyse how the team are going to manage data integrity on the contact object to avoid issues in the future. Secondly consider a range of strategies from data capture tools to validation rules, and trusted data sources, to populate and maintain clean data.

Data Compliance

Analyse the KPIs you will use to assess consent compliance and integrity in the system, alongside assessing your data protection policies.

Consent Management

To align with data protection, it is essential to track the history of consent fields on the contact object, ensuring you maintain records demonstrating compliance. Data protection rules will vary internationally but here are some key consent fields you should track history on:

Salesforce out of the box only allows you to track history on 20 fields per object so to achieve data protection requirements you might need to look at alternative ISV apps such as Processity.

Key Consent Fields to Track History on:

Identity of the Data Subject: name, email, or any other unique identifier of the individual giving consent.

Date and Time of Consent: the exact timestamp when consent was given or withdrawn.

Form and Method of Consent: whether consent was given electronically, in writing, or verbally, and the specific mechanism used (e.g., checkbox on a web form).

Specifics of Consent: details on what exactly the individual consented to, such as specific data processing activities, purposes, and the types of data being collected.

Version of Consent Text: the exact wording of the consent statement at the time of consent, including any privacy policy or terms referenced.

Source of Consent: the context or platform where consent was given (e.g., website, mobile app, in-person).

Withdrawal of Consent: records of when and how consent was withdrawn, if applicable.

Recommended Duration for Retaining Consent Records

Under GDPR, there is no specific duration mandated for retaining consent records. However, you should keep consent records for as long as the data is being processed and as long as necessary to demonstrate compliance with GDPR. Here are some practical guidelines:

Active Processing: retain consent records for as long as you are processing the data subject's information based on that consent.

Post-Processing: after you stop processing the data, retain the consent records for a reasonable period to demonstrate compliance, typically for the statute of limitations for any legal claims (commonly three to six years, depending on the jurisdiction).

Withdrawal of Consent: if consent is withdrawn, retain the record of the original consent and the withdrawal for a reasonable period, as evidence of your compliance and the actions taken.

Best Practices

Data Minimisation: only retain consent records that are necessary for demonstrating compliance.

Regular Reviews: periodically review and securely delete consent records that are no longer needed.

Security: ensure that consent records are stored securely to prevent unauthorised access and breaches.

Audit Trails: maintain detailed audit trails to provide a clear history of consent actions.

By diligently tracking and retaining these consent fields, you can ensure compliance with GDPR requirements and be prepared to demonstrate your data protection practices if audited or challenged.

Thank you to Processity for sponsoring this chapter. Audicity by *processity.ai.* Boost Salesforce efficiency with unlimited field history. Audicity enables tracking as many standard and custom objects as required, and as many fields on those objects as you need. It offers process insights on interconnected events in Salesforce, all while maintaining effortless configuration.

MANAGING DATA QUALITY

Within this chapter we provide an introduction to managing data quality. In the age of digital transformation, data has become one of the most valuable assets for businesses. Leveraging data effectively can provide insights that drive decision-making, enhance customer experiences, and fuel innovation.

Poor data quality is also one of the biggest reasons why CRMs are not adopted, because users don't trust the data.

Poor data governance can impact the organisation significantly[2]:

- Inaccurate or incomplete data can lead to 20 percent stalled productivity, which is one day of work each week.
- The average company loses 12 percent of its revenue as a result of inaccurate data.
- 40 percent of all business initiatives fail to achieve their

---

[2] Data Governance PDF https://a.sfdcstatic.com/content/dam/www/ocms-backup/assets/pdf/misc/data_Governance_Stewardship_ebook.pdf

targeted benefits because of poor-quality data.

Bad data is consistently linked with lost revenue, missing or inaccurate insights, wasted time and resources, inefficiency, poor customer service, slow retrieval of information, reputational damage and decreased adoption by reps.

Good data lets your organisation prospect and target new customers, identify cross-sell and upsell opportunities, gain account insights, increase efficiency, retrieve the right info fast, build trust with customers, increase adoption by reps, plan and align territories better and score and route leads faster.

Find out what data is important to your management team.

The 80/20 rule is often cited as applying to your data for example 20 percent of your fields will be the most important in your organisation to align with performance management dashboards, AI automation, compliance. Conduct a business analysis workshop to discover:

- What are the business objectives?
- What customer data is required to support those objectives?
- How are they currently using that customer data?
- Where is the customer data stored?

Summarise the most important fields that are necessary to support business intelligence and define these as the compulsory or core fields. Going forward you want to maintain oversight on the data integrity of these fields to ensure they are being populated successfully.

To achieve this, you need to assess the data quality of these fields and analyse where problems may lie, then resolve any issues through clear business rules and/or technical features to improve population through automation.

Assess Data Quality

Once you have a summary of the most important data fields, it's time to assess the quality of this data using tools such as DemandTools from Validity:

- Age – when was each record last updated?
- Completeness – are all key business fields on records filled in?
- Accuracy – is your data as accurate as possible? Has it been matched against a trusted source?
- Consistency – is the same formatting, spelling, and language used across records?
- Duplication – are records and data duplicated in your org?
- Usage – is your data being harnessed in reports, dashboards, and apps?
- Cleansing – is data no longer required in the system being deleted?

Data Management

Once you've analysed the most important data requirements and appraised the current situation, we recommend that clear business rules are agreed by your team and communicated during training about which data is collected and required in the system at different stages of the customer journey.

Where possible, you want to harness Salesforce technical features and apps to automatically improve data capture, population and reduce data integrity issues.

To support data management here are some recommendations you could take forward:

- Naming – set naming conventions for records. Always include suffixes (Inc., Corp.)? Abbreviations?
- Formatting – figure out how dates and money are represented.
- Workflow/flows – determine processes for record creation, reviewing, updating, and archiving. Determine all the stages a record goes through during its life cycle.
- Security and permissions – determine the appropriate levels of privacy for data. Make sure to comply with regulatory, legal, and contractual obligations.
- Monitoring reports and dashboards – outline a process for ensuring quality control of data. Determine the frequency, scope, owners, and checks, including ways for updating data, preventing duplicates, merging

records, adding records, and archiving records. Determine metrics that can be easily monitored in a dashboard.

- Paths – provide clarity/guidance to users about what data to input during each stage of a customer journey by using Paths on the object.
- Required fields – make sure fields are required that support your business objectives.
- Validation rules – set up validation rules for any field. Then, when records are saved, the data is checked to make sure it follows the format.
- Page layouts – remove fields from the page layout for team members that don't need or use them and put the most important, required fields at the top.
- Data enrichment tools – data is obsolete almost as soon as it's entered. That's why it's important to regularly match your data against a trusted source.
- Duplicate management – identify duplicate rules and determine the best approach for identifying new ones or managing existing ones. This could be using the native Duplicate Management tool or a third-party app.
- Custom field types – create custom field types to help standardise data collection where data is inconsistent and can't be analysed.

HARNESSING DATA ANALYTICS

Within this chapter we do a deep dive into data analytics and explore what Salesforce CRM Analytics is and why businesses invest in it beyond standard reports and dashboards to improve their data intelligence and security.

The goal is to use analysed data to make better-informed, customer-conscious business decisions. CRM analytics is an incredible tool for businesses of all sizes, but it is especially vital for large organisations that deal with an enormous number of customers a day. With so many different customers it can be tricky for those in sales, customer service, marketing, and any department who might be involved to keep track of where each customer is at each stage of their process.

CRM analytics allows you to build the bridge between the numbers and the clients, allowing companies to view their most important connections, gaps, and risks associated with every customer action. Salesforce CRM Analytics is a powerful cloud-based analytics and business intelligence (BI) solution on the Salesforce platform.

Salesforce CRM Analytics, formerly known as Tableau, Einstein Analytics and Wave, is an astute, accurate, and extensive CRM analytics solution, designed to allow users to combine customer data from a plethora of data sources and transform this into valuable insights.

What are the benefits of Salesforce CRM Analytics?

The data you gather regarding your customers needs to be extensive and precise, allowing you to customise your strategy and be aligned to the individuals that make up your customer base, rather than a generic all-encompassing approach. Every customer wants to feel valued, and CRM Analytics allows you to do that. Here are some more benefits:

Customer Classification

CRM analytics tools also make it possible to segment your clients into various groups, such as those based on age, gender, spending habits, buying trends etc., for smoother marketing and sales management. This enhances the customer 360-degree view with real time data.

Predictive Monitoring No Coding

The declarative tool can analyse customer data to accurately determine how successful future business decisions may be, reducing the overall risk and increasing sales potential. Accessing a wide range of data sources and housing this dataset inside the analytics studio can identify trends and patterns to effectively predict future outcomes.

Identify Quality Records

CRM sales analytics are designed to determine which groups of customers are likely to bring in the highest ROI utilising customer segmentation. This allows businesses to focus more of their advertising, marketing, and sales efforts on the most valuable demographics, ensuring higher profits over time. The data enables the sales reps to pursue the high opportunity sales deals.

Native to Salesforce

Everything in CRM Analytics adheres to Salesforce's number one value - trust - and therefore security. CRM Analytics also simplifies data governance, allowing you to adapt to new business requirements as user adoption and engagement evolve. You can adopt existing Salesforce security or create bespoke accessibility and manage internally.

Why do Businesses Invest in Salesforce CRM Analytics?

CRM Analytics allows companies to view their most important connections, gaps, and risks associated with every customer action. Benefits include:

Data Integration

Salesforce CRM Analytics allows businesses to integrate data from various sources, including customer interactions, sales transactions, and marketing campaigns. This enables organisations to gain a comprehensive view of their operations and make data-driven decisions. In business decision-making, actionable intelligence makes it mandatory to merge data from various systems. Users can connect the CRM software with survey data with multiple ERPs to increase sales productivity and improve service quality.

CRM Analytics now includes built-in connectivity to all types of data sources, such as Google BigQuery, SAP, AWS, CSV Files, etc. It becomes convenient for users to connect with non-Salesforce data and process all these at the centre.

Use article recommendations for getting the right information.

CRM Analytics hasn't restricted its capabilities in providing apt responses, but its learnings can be used in various service scenarios. Let's take knowledge articles as an example. You might have encountered this incident on Salesforce's customer support hub, where Blaze comes in with many knowledge articles.

Salesforce CRM Analytics jumps into action by identifying the right information for your requirements. Customers can also find the appropriate info by self-servicing faster and more accurately. With Einstein intelligence, you no longer have to scroll through an entire knowledge base or struggle with finding the right content by conducting keyword searches.

Automatically retrieving more recommendations and insights.

With traditional analytical approaches, users easily understand what happened in the past and the reason behind it to make the right future predictions. Einstein-AI backed-up analytics gives you a clear picture of the future and foresee how things can go.

Utilise the next best action for determining the best course.

One of the key features of Salesforce Einstein Analytics is recognising the best course of action through Predictive Intelligence while keeping users on a live interaction with a customer. It helps users deliver the maximum impact on customer interactions at crucial checkpoints. For instance, recommending any best-suited cross-selling opportunity, such as an add-on warranty, while resolving the case.

Trail every activity of the user with event monitoring analytics.

Every minute detail of user activity can be tracked with event monitoring analytics, parallel providing security to data. Businesses can view all kinds of activity detail about the individual event and identify changing behavioural patterns so that data can be safeguarded on time.

Event monitoring empowers teams to track logins, logouts, Lightning (web clicks, performance, errors in Lightning Experiences and The Salesforce Mobile App), URI (web clicks in Salesforce Classic), API calls, Apex executions, Reports exports, and more.

Interactive Dashboards

With Salesforce CRM Analytics, users can create interactive dashboards that display real-time data in a visually appealing format. This allows stakeholders to easily identify trends, patterns, and areas of concern.

Customisable Reports

Salesforce CRM Analytics provides users with the ability to create custom reports that are tailored to their specific needs. Reports can be generated on a scheduled basis or as needed, providing users with up-to-date information.

Mobile Access

Salesforce CRM Analytics is accessible on mobile devices, allowing users to access data and insights on-the-go. This enables stakeholders to make informed decisions regardless of their location.

By the end of this chapter, you should understand how Salesforce CRM Analytics can help businesses use their CRM data to achieve their goals. It can provide insights, predictions, and recommendations that can help sales and service teams make data-driven decisions. CRM Analytics can also help businesses:

- Identify trends and problems.
- understand customer needs and behaviours.
- enhance customer relationships and loyalty; and
- optimise marketing campaigns.

Embrace the power of Salesforce CRM Analytics today and unlock new possibilities for your business and career. With CRM Analytics, the future of data management and analytics is within your reach.

Thank you to Nebula Consulting for sponsoring this chapter.

Nebula helps businesses gain, maintain and sell to customers and communicate with stakeholders via the Salesforce ecosystem. Specialisms include CRM Analytics, Sales Cloud, Revenue Cloud, Account Engagement and Communities.

CRM ROADMAP

Within this section we delve into the fun admin tasks of building the CRM Roadmap to keep the business, users, and system advancing with different products to improve performance and efficiencies. In this role you are the innovator with the opportunity to research and propose new solutions to transform the business and ways of working.

The creation of the CRM Roadmap requires a combination of skills including business analysis and Agile project management to discover what is needed, to assess the return on investment, and to prioritise what happens first.

A Salesforce CRM system will never be 'finished'. There are always opportunities for improvements and advancements as new technology products and functionality evolves.

Within this section we are going to equip you with an

introduction to business analysis and Agile project management skills, tools and templates to gather and prioritise requirements.

To get started it's important to do an initial review with the management team to review the current business vision and challenges. During this review you will want to:

- Review the three-year business plan for the organisation.
- Evaluate the biggest challenges to or opportunities for realising the business ambitions.
- Appraise the technical products that can add the most value.
- Assess the return on investment of implementing these products.
- Build the business case for the CRM Roadmap.

Within the following chapters we take a deep dive into:

- Centre of Excellence – how to set up a governance structure for investing in the CRM.
- KPIs for measuring ROI – how to evaluate the return on investment of products.
- Agile Project Management – how to prioritise requirements and manage budgets.
- Business Analysis – how to gather and record requirements.

Here is a quick summary of the to do list.

Weekly/Daily	Monthly	Quarterly
Agile Project Management	Business Analysis	Centre of Excellence
	KPIs for Measuring ROI	

CENTRE OF EXCELLENCE

Within this chapter we explore the importance and value of setting up a Centre of Excellence (CoE) to support your role as a Salesforce Administrator.

A Salesforce CoE basically acts as a central governing body for the entire organisation. It brings together stakeholders from across the organisation to create a single, well-defined group that is responsible for making decisions when it comes to Salesforce.

How to Establish a Salesforce Centre of Excellence (CoE)

To achieve success, the Salesforce CoE is responsible for allocating suitable resources and helping to determine priorities for investment and time needed to achieve this by the technical team.

Without an effective Salesforce CoE, you may struggle to achieve:

- Prioritisation of requests and workload
- Sign-off for new products, features and requirements

- Secured budget and resources
- Buy-in from different teams/departments
- A clear CRM road map
- Reporting on the ROI
- Optimal user adoption.

A CoE creates a good governance structure to support the ongoing planning, management and maintenance of your Salesforce system.

The CoE is responsible for the CRM Strategy, managing governance and setting and evaluating the metrics of success. To achieve success, it is responsible for allocating suitable resources and helping to determine priorities for investment and time needed by the technical team. Typically, the group would meet monthly or quarterly depending on the level of transformation taking place.

What Are Some of the Essential Ingredients for a Salesforce Centre of Excellence?

CRM Strategy, Roadmap & Action Plan

The CRM Strategy clearly outlines the business case and performance metrics the CRM is expected to support with stages of implementation and justification for investment. It should facilitate decision making to create a detailed road map, agreed deliverables and a clear progress report on ROI. It is also great to use as a communication tool, as it serves as a high-level document that helps articulate strategic thinking (the why) behind both the goal, and the plan for getting there, to stakeholders.

Cross-Departmental Team Input

A CoE requires a cross-departmental decision-making team with bottom-up and top-down representation.

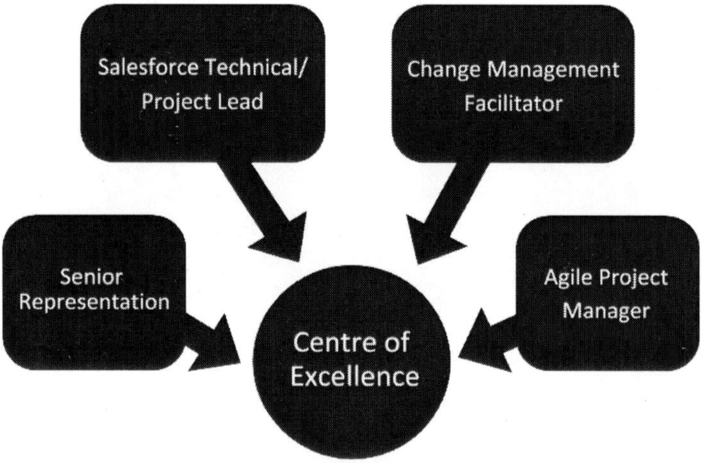

- An internal leader should be appointed as the executive sponsor. They will typically lead the CoE representing the business vision, goals, and priorities.
- Senior management representatives who are responsible for sponsorship, business analysis, compliance and/or adoption of Salesforce CRM within their department or cross-departments.

- Salesforce Technical/Project Lead who will have oversight of the roadmap, project development and the backlog informed by on the ground business analysis and the technical implementation team. They are responsible for communicating new requirements, agreeing prioritisation, and reporting on work in progress or completed.
- Agile Project Management Lead who will manage what, when and how things will be scheduled for implementation with oversight of internal and external influences.
- Change Management Lead who will manage a communication strategy to communicate the why, what and when of digital transformation changes, with input from senior exec level representatives to the Salesforce team.

Investment in Business Analysis

The Salesforce technical/project lead will prepare for these meetings by collating high level requirements, estimating effort, and the associated business case by working closing with a delivery team. Individuals may wear one or more hats in this function, but the common roles are:

- Salesforce champions are representatives within departments who oversee user adoption, identify challenges, uncover requirements, and report these to the senior managers.

- Business analysts elicit detailed requirements with teams/departments to produce the business case and requirement log.
- The Salesforce technical team is responsible for building and managing the system day to day to understand progress, challenges, and outcomes.

The Role of an Executive Sponsor

The CoE needs a strong executive sponsor who understands their role and responsibilities with an emphasis on allocating resources and ensuring there is clear communication strategy about the business case and timelines to C-Suite, managers and the front-line. The executive sponsor's communication strategy is instrumental to the change management strategy. Great communication leads to high engagement, and high engagement leads to great design that optimises benefits and ensures high adoption.

By the end of this chapter, you should understand what support you need around you as a Salesforce Administrator to achieve your deliverables.

KPIS FOR MEASURING RETURN ON INVESTMENT (ROI)

Within this chapter, we focus on how to calculate the return on investment of your Salesforce CRM and demonstrate that the value exceeds the related expenditure to the business.

If a business is investing in Salesforce products, it's important to build a clear business case and ROI. Determining the value of a CRM system like Salesforce requires effort but it is necessary to justify expenses as well as ensure successful strategies and business growth.

How to Measure Improvements

To be able to calculate and demonstrate ROI, you'll need to have ways of identifying and measuring the improvements that result from the Salesforce CRM.

To achieve this, you need to:

1. Identify the drivers for organisational and departmental change.
2. Define tangible (with a clear monetary value) and intangible benefits (other improvements).

3. Review your current baseline statistics.
4. Agree your goals for the future.
5. Define SMART (specific, measurable, achievable, realistic, time-framed) measures of success.

Below are some example Key Performance Indicators (KPIs) you could use in different areas:

Customer service:

- Improved feedback score
- Increase in impact and outcomes
- Improved referral rates

Stakeholder engagement:

- Improved engagement rates
- Increase in ROI in campaigns
- Improved retention rates

Efficiency:

- Reduced costs
- Achieved quality standards
- Reduced leakage

Business intelligence:

- Ideas for continual improvement
- New innovations
- Improved marketing proposition

Financial sustainability:

- Quicker customer conversion
- Increased revenue
- Improved financial assurance.

Let's delve into the five main indicator areas in a bit more depth.

Customer service

Has the business invested in Salesforce to improve the customer service experience? To measure its impact, we recommend tracking customer feedback scores to look for potential improvements, such as an increase in repeat customers or referral rates. The better the insights into how your customers respond to your products, services and support, the more likely you are to ensure customer satisfaction in the future.

Stakeholder engagement rates

If the business has adopted Salesforce to improve customer relationships, it's important you are accurately capturing contact information and preferences. Once you have engaged with your customers and are communicating to them in their preferred way, you can track any improvement in engagement rates, an increase in ROI of marketing campaigns and, hopefully, improve retention rates.

Business efficiency

Does the business plan to use Salesforce to save time and money as well as allocate resources into more profitable activities? Quite often, businesses use automation tools to automatically capture stakeholder information and automate responses to reduce administrative burden. If so, you will benefit from measuring any reduction in costs and time and potentially leakage too.

Business intelligence

Capturing customer and employee feedback, including their ideas and suggestions, can be a great way to plan future business strategies, product updates, marketing campaigns and more. In addition, with this information you can demonstrate how Salesforce has helped you capture new ideas for continual development or improved market proposition.

Financial sustainability

Another reason why businesses invest in Salesforce and third-party apps is because they want to convert customers faster. To achieve this, you need the ability to streamline online product purchases while keeping any contact or payment information secure.

How to calculate the ROI

Calculating the ROI of the new Salesforce CRM requires you to first estimate then compare the expected cost of development and operation with the benefits of making the change once it's complete.

ROI = expected average annual profit × 100 / total investment

For example: (50,000 / 5) × 100 / 100,000 = 10%

At the end of this chapter, you should be able to mobilise your client to identify the most relevant KPIs to measure and demonstrate the ROI of their digital transformation project and present a solid business case for continued investment.

Thank you to Frankly Solutions for sponsoring this chapter. Frankly are a specialised Salesforce consulting partner, helping customers maximise the value of their investment in the Salesforce ecosystem.□Frankly Solutions brings many person-years of Salesforce implementation experience, gained at enterprise-level companies,□to bear on projects of all shapes and sizes.□They can help you with your Salesforce journey. □

AGILE PROJECT MANAGEMENT

Within this chapter you will learn more about Agile PM, why it's important, what its value is and why it is the norm for tech projects.

If you are prioritising your workload, you will need a methodology for doing this that everyone can align to. As the Salesforce Administrator your responsibility is to fulfil technical solutions that support business needs and your prioritisation of tasks should align to business priorities informed by management.

It's important to understand and get trained up in Agile Dynamic Systems Development Method (DSDM) project management so you feel confident delivering this methodology on a project.

What is Agile PM?

Agile PM evolved in the '90s with a specific focus on technology projects; since then, organisations large and small have embraced the new age of 'Agile'.

There are four key things to understand about Agile PM:

1. 'Agile project management' is an umbrella term for a variety of different methods – the DSDM, Scrum and Lean are some examples.
2. Agile focuses on prioritisation and iteration of flexible requirements, working within time and budget constraints using MoSCoW prioritisation.
3. Agile is now considered the norm for technology projects.
4. Agile is a global project management practice, with tools and systems to manage requirements, time and costs.

Why is Agile PM Important and Valuable?

If there's a long wish list of requirements and demands with no prioritisation or project management, you will find it a challenge to meet the expectations of clients and teams. This can lead to frustration on all sides, and will result in:

- Requirements not being correctly prioritised and budget spent in the wrong areas
- Half-baked solutions
- Technology not aligning to business need
- Overspend on budget
- Timeframes not being met

Organisations are increasingly embracing Agile as a technique for managing projects. A recent global survey found that 71 percent of organisations report using Agile approaches for their projects sometimes, often or always.[3]

A report by APMG showed that the greater the utilisation of Agile methods in a project, the more successful that project is in meeting all its aims.[4]

Senior executives increasingly recognise that Agile is 'eating the world'.[5]

In fact, surveys by both Deloitte and McKinsey show that over 90 percent of senior executives want to be Agile, while less than 10 percent currently see their own firm as 'highly agile'. There are now major efforts underway with 'Agile transformations' being planned or implemented in many organisations, both public and private. All the successful software firms are recognisably implementing the substance of Agile – a focus on delivering value for customers, working in small teams in short cycles, and networked organisational

---

[3] PMI *Pulse of the Profession: 9th Global Project Management Survey* (PMI, 2017) www.pmi.org/-/media/pmi/documents/public/pdf/learning/thought-leadership/pulse/pulse-of-the-profession-2017.pdf

[4] P Serrador and JK Pinto, 'Does Agile work? A quantitative analysis of Agile project success', *International*

[5] Denning, S, 'Agile Is Not Just Another Management Fad' *Forbes* (30 July 2018), www.forbes.com/sites/stevedenning/2018/07/30/agile- is-not-just-another-management-fad/?sh=571a4ea31957, accessed 4 September 2023

arrangements rather than top-down bureaucracy and silos.[6]

Why is Agile PM the Norm in Tech?

This comes down to practicalities. In the context of technology agencies and projects, rarely is there a detailed technical specification designed upfront, so it's usually impossible, or at least high risk, for agencies to give a fixed price on a project when requirements are unknown. Technology is advancing all the time and market conditions are ever-changing, meaning there may be a need to evolve solutions and requirements as needed throughout the lifetime of the project.

Often, the users don't know or understand the technical features available at the outset of the project, so the Agile process provides the user with the flexibility to evolve their requirements throughout the project as they learn more about their approach.

Quick wins build confidence, so if you can develop a system in stages this will allow users to see and celebrate success in earlier stages without committing to a whole project.

Typically, there is a fixed budget for a project (with contingency). It is in the best interests of both parties to deliver on high-priority requirements within this budget, without compromising the working relationship or quality. This reduces

---

[6] Ibid.

the risk as they can choose to allocate and spend resources as needed rather than stick rigidly to an upfront plan.

In Agile DSDM project management:

- Budget and time are fixed and agreed upfront but can be increased.
- Requirements are prioritised throughout and aligned to business need.
- There is an iterative process where design, build, test and roll-out happen throughout.
- Flexibility is key throughout the project life cycle.

Which Agile PM Methodology Suits your Job Role?

As mentioned, there are various methods within the umbrella term of 'Agile' PM, but the two main ones are DSDM and Scrum.

DSDM

DSDM is an Agile method that focuses on the full project life cycle.[7]

DSDM was developed in 1994, after project managers using RAD (rapid application development) sought more governance

[7] More information about DSDM can be found at www.agilebusiness.org/dsdm-project-framework.html

and discipline in this new, iterative way of working.

DSDM's success is due to the philosophy that 'any project must be aligned to clearly defined strategic goals and focus upon early delivery of real benefits to the business'.[8]

This philosophy is supported by eight principles that allow teams to maintain focus and achieve the project goals.

The eight principles of DSDM:

- Focus on the business need
- Deliver on time
- Collaborate
- Never compromise quality
- Build incrementally from firm foundations
- Develop iteratively
- Communicate continuously and clearly
- Demonstrate control.

The DSDM approach is the best methodology if you manage CRM implementations at a strategic level, working with the executive team and managing both the business analysis and technical team. It helps you to see the big picture and prioritise projects, tasks and requirements. This would suit a Salesforce project manager or solo Salesforce Administrator/system

[8] www.agilebusiness.org/business-agility/what-is-dsdm.html

manager.

DSDM uses MoSCoW Rules to prioritise requirements with the categorisation of 'Must Have, Should Have, Could Have, Won't Have' at a tiered level – starting with the business need, to high level requirements to more detailed technical requirements.

DSDM may also be used to supplement an existing in-house Agile approach, where this has proved to be lacking. For example, DSDM is often used to provide the full project focus to complement Scrum's team focused product development process.

Scrum

Scrum is the best methodology if you have been given a sub-set of technical requirements and you are managing a technical team to implement those requirements on a daily basis. This method would best suit a Salesforce technical lead who is managing the daily build of a solution.

At the end of this chapter, you should have a better understanding of why Agile PM is so valuable, and of the role it plays in managing expectations related to a project and improving communication with customers on deliverables.

BUSINESS ANALYSIS

This chapter will provide an introduction into business analysis (BA) outlining why it is important and what it entails.

Introduction to business analysis

In a LinkedIn poll we posted, 43 percent voted poor BA as the biggest risk to Salesforce projects[9], and this concern is echoed within industry reports.

Recent research has found that, on average, performance virtually doubled as organisations progressed from using an ad-hoc approach for requirements definition and management to having institutionalised and consistent competency in all capability areas. The research highlighted the following stats:[10]

- Average on-time performance of technology projects increased by 161 percent

---

[9] www.linkedin.com/posts/heather-black-salesforce-women-in- tech-speaker_salesforce-activity-7046012463007285248-0EYJ?utm_source=share&utm_medium=member_desktop, accessed 4 September 2023

[10] IAG Consulting, 'Business Analysis Benchmark – Full Report', www.iag.biz/resource/business-analysis-benchmark-full-report, accessed 4 September 2023

- Time overruns on projects reduced by 87 percent
- Average on-budget performance for technology projects improved by just over 95 percent
- Budget overruns reduced by just under 75 percent
- Percentage of projects that deliver the functionality needed by the business rose by just over 75 percent
- Average functionality missed dropped by approximately 78 percent

BA isn't a standalone discipline; however, it must be interwoven with Agile PM and change management skills to be fully effective. This is because, when the BA workshops uncover hundreds of requirements, you need to know how to prioritise them, with the input of the client, using Agile DSDM project management.

This prioritisation requires that you know the most pressing business priorities and ROI expectations so they can be aligned.

The stakeholders also need to be engaged, enthused and empowered during the BA process. Adopting appropriate change management techniques during BA elicitation is key to generating buy-in during the design period and training workshops.

What is a Business Analyst?

Within the Salesforce world, a business analyst is someone who analyses a business process, identifies the pain points and helps the client to prioritise areas that can be improved using technology.

Business analysis techniques are great skills to have in any Salesforce-related job role, whether it's sales, admin, consultant, architect or straight business analyst, of course. Why? Because technology will only be successful if it is solving a business need and helping the company, team or individual perform better.

In order for a technology transformation project to be successful, it is imperative that:

- Processes are reviewed in detail and improved
- Priorities are scrutinised and agreed
- Technology options are appraised
- Goals and outcomes are measurable and clear.

The four principles of BA are summarised in the POPIT decision-making model:

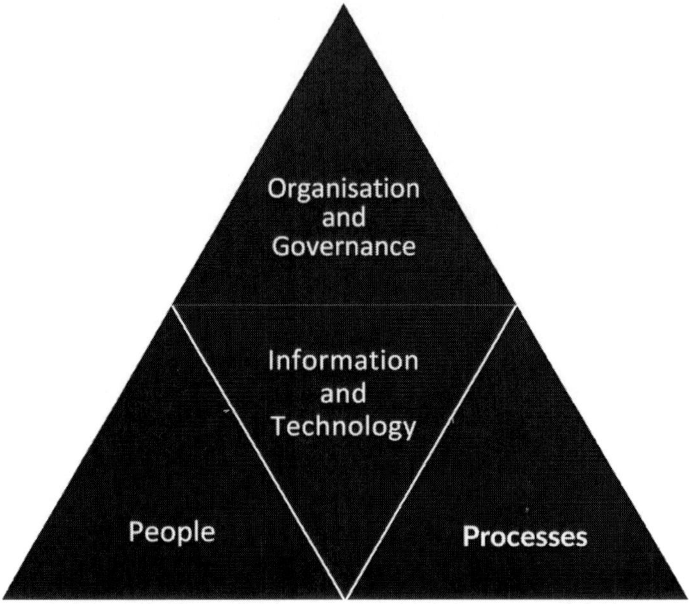

- **People:** you need to assess the skills and needs of the stakeholders involved – what are their needs, pain points and aspirations?
- **Organisation & Governance:** you also need to assess the business, its strategy, its culture and what it is striving to achieve.
- **Processes:** assess the current state of the processes and determine the aspirations for improving and refining these processes to meet the needs of the people and the organisation.
- **Information and Technology:** assess the current technology use and identify future possible needs based

on the people, organisation and processes to determine the best solutions to meet those needs.

Agreeing the CRM Strategy

A roadmap is a strategic plan that defines a goal or the desired outcome, which includes the major steps or milestones needed to reach it. It is also great to use as a communication tool, as it serves as a high-level document that helps articulate strategic thinking (the why) behind both the goal and the plan for getting there to stakeholders.

It should map out the CRM roll-out across and between departments, and the implementation of different Salesforce and independent software vendor (ISV) products, to deliver on the desired business objectives and priorities.

It is important to have a CRM roadmap because, if there aren't clear priorities, the CoE and Salesforce delivery team won't have a North Star to focus on. They won't know what to work on first to best improve the situation of the business, its employees and customers. Without this clarity, the Salesforce technical team can feel overwhelmed, and attention can be focused on the wrong areas, hampering the project's ability to meet the needs of the organisation.

The Salesforce delivery team member(s) need to have the professional skills of BA, Agile PM and change management to effectively facilitate the conversations needed to produce a

CRM roadmap. Without this, there will be poor system adoption, integration and alignment across departments, resulting in data silos, poor customer intelligence and inconsistent information across systems. All of this undermines the value placed on the CRM and can lead to low adoption of the system.

How to Plan a CRM Roadmap

Understanding the strategic business priorities is the first step to determining the priorities of a CRM build; this helps to lay the foundation for creating the CRM strategy. Applying Agile project management methodologies is the most common approach used for prioritisation in technology projects. This foundation can only be put in place if there is a clear governance structure for the CRM; this is commonly called a centre of excellence (CoE) and is hosted by an executive sponsor.

Project governance is a crucial element of the CRM roadmap, especially for complicated and risky projects. You need a framework for making decisions about the project, defining roles, responsibilities and liabilities for the accomplishment of the project, and that governs the effectiveness of the delivery.

Preparation for Business Analysis

Properly preparing the stakeholders for a business analysis workshop is a game changer, as it increases the amount of time they invest in planning and designing so that you can be confident you're building the right solution.

As part of this preparation, you should meet with the key sponsors and executive team to understand and prioritise the main business drivers for this implementation and to decide on the approach you are collectively going to take to elicit requirements from stakeholders.

Understanding the business priorities will help to prioritise functional and technical requirements. A change management and communication plan are also essential, and your approach to BA will be governed by the organisational culture and preferred communication style of the executive team.

The main things you need to cover with stakeholders are:

- Advise and work with the executive sponsor on how and when to implement a suitable communication strategy to inform the stakeholders about the why, what and how of the Salesforce project, to generate buy-in.
- Explain the BA and Agile PM process in advance of a discovery workshop to anyone who is participating. Showcase a demo of the product features, explain the questions you are going to ask and how requirements can be prioritised. Record this session so people can

rewatch it as needed.

- Agree a suitable timeline by which the participants will prepare all of the information you will need before the discovery workshop, to maximise its value. There is no point running a workshop if participants turn up unprepared without the answers to your questions. This is often one of the biggest causes of project delays and budget impacts.
- Circulate a BA questionnaire in advance of the discovery workshop with a deadline for participants to complete it by, so you can review their responses before conducting the workshop and to make sure the relevant information has been prepared. You can access a whole set of business analysis questionnaires on our Consultancy Skills course.

During the discovery workshop, present different technical scenarios and a demo to help improve processes so that participants can make informed decisions.

To make this easy for you, we have developed a four-step approach to business analysis.

Follow this and you'll be a BA pro. There are also various templates (BA questionnaires and documentation) available within the Supermums Consultancy Skills course.

1. Understand the why – what is the strategy underpinning the business case for the CRM implementation?

- Understand the business strategy
- Complete a SWOT analysis
- Identify the KPIs
- Mobilise the roles and responsibilities of the executive sponsor
- Establish a centre of excellence
- Identify the business stakeholders who need to be consulted

2. Understand how the client works and what they need, then execute your BA elicitation strategy with different stakeholders. This could include:

- Delivering demos
- Interviews
- Shadowing
- Workshops
- Questionnaires
- Meetings
- Focus groups
- Document analysis

3. Record the business needs in a professional way to provide clear documentation. A suite of BA documentation would include:

- Business canvas, explaining the business strategy.
- Business case, demonstrating the ROI for the CRM
- CRM strategy, outlining the reasons and strategy for the CRM.
- Process maps, documenting the before and after business processes.
- Technical audit, documenting the different technology used by a business and how it interacts.
- Stakeholder context diagram, showcasing the different stakeholders and their interaction with the various systems.
- Requirements log, detailing the functional, non-functional and technical requirements with the level of prioritisation and business case.
- Technical workbook, detailing all of the elements that need to be built by a technical team.
- Object entity diagram, showcasing the high- level architecture of the CRM system.

4. Schedule when to do BA and the CRM implementation with an agreed project management plan. Here are some questions to find answers to:

- What are the functional requirements?
- What are the non-functional requirements?

- What is the MoSCoW prioritisation of requirements in line with DSDM Agile PM?
- What is the time frame to completing the requirements?
- What are the dependencies between the requirements?
- What is the budget for the overall implementation?
- What is the resource for the overall implementation?

To help get you started we have equipped you with some initial business analysis questions to consider when conducting a Sales Cloud, Service Cloud, E-Marketing or Fundraising Design workshop. Check out the following chapters and download the technical tests from the Book Resource Page.

SCAN ME

At the end of this chapter, you should have a better understanding of why business analysis is important and what the different approaches to gathering requirements can be.

This chapter is kindly sponsored by CUBE84. CUBE84 is a full-service Salesforce consulting company that can solve your most challenging projects. Whether it's a full-blown implementation of Salesforce from scratch or a simple audit of your existing configuration, their Salesforce consultants are here to help you make the most of your CRM investment. From understanding business goals to implementing robust solutions, they have got you covered with a holistic team of Solution Architects, Project Managers, Business Analysts, Administrators, and Developers. A Certified Salesforce Partner since 2015.

BUSINESS ANALYSIS FOR SALES CLOUD

Within this chapter we give a high-level overview of what to consider during the Sales Cloud discovery process.

Typically, a Sales Cloud implementation will include the following high level requirements:

1. Online payments – do they have one-off, recurring or multiple transactions and which integrated payment solution will meet their needs?
2. Sealing the deal – from lead to sale how can this process be automated to speed up the quote to contract sign-off process with integrated apps?
3. Managing the funnel – what are the lead to opportunity stages and activities throughout the sales funnel and how do you maximise Sales Cloud functionality?
4. Monitoring progress – how do you schedule and log activities, collaborate with colleagues and partners and monitor performance of the sales team?
5. From sales to finance – how do you co-ordinate sales to finance management to ensure seamless management?

Within the Supermums Consultancy Skills course, we provide a full business analysis questionnaire for Sales Cloud, online payments, and non-functional requirements with a presentation deck and a training session on how to deliver it alongside the technical considerations. If you are worried about what questions to ask, then check out our course.

Here are five of the favourite questions you don't want to miss but there are loads more functional and non-functional requirement questions that you want to include in your questionnaire:

- What are their different products, services and customers? Are there multiple sales teams? And where are their teams and customers located, globally? This will influence how many different project life cycles you will need to deliver e.g., multiple discovery workshops through to training sessions and also whether global influences are relevant such as languages and currency considerations.
- What are the pain points and key benefits they want to derive from Salesforce as a sales team from different points of view – as an organisation, a team and individually?
- How would the company measure the ROI of the Salesforce investment? What are the baseline stats now and what do they want them to be in the future? It can be useful to have some example indicators here to share in case they aren't sure. For example, increase in

conversion time, increase in repeat customers, increase in conversion of leads funnel, increase in lead rating ratio, increase in calls booked.

- How is sales performance measured? What are their key reports and dashboard requirements as they will influence how you build the system? Again, it can be useful to have some example indicators here to share in case they aren't sure. e.g., number of calls booked per week, number of converted leads, value of closed deals, number of deals in the pipeline, against targets.
- What is their sales process? Within this there will be multiple functional questions ask and technical considerations to address, especially to discover whether the Sales Cloud functionality needs extending to integrate with third-party apps to integrate online payments, e-signature contracts or reconcile with accounting software. This will inevitably increase time and budget for any project.

As a Salesforce Administrator you will want to understand the different scenarios and technical solutions to propose to a client during the business analysis session.

Download our Sales Cloud technical tests from the Book Resources page to check your knowledge around a Sales Cloud implementation and get clear on what scenarios to put on the table during the business analysis workshop.

SCAN ME

Thank you to Rocketphone.Ai for sponsoring this chapter. RocketPhone.ai empowers organisations to unlock the full potential of their customer conversations by transforming them into actionable insights. They bring clarity to businesses by capturing and unifying every interaction—whether through mobile calls, contact centres, or video calls—into a single, centralised system of record. The RocketPhone.ai platform leverages advanced AI to contextualise conversations, surface real-time insights, and drive impactful decisions and workflows. They enable organisations to enhance productivity, increase revenue predictability, and make smarter decisions that fuel business growth.

BUSINESS ANALYSIS FOR SERVICE CLOUD

Within this chapter we give a high-level overview of what to consider during the Service Cloud discovery process.

Typically, a Service Cloud implementation will include the following high-level requirements:

Customer Engagement – How do you engage customers and capture their support requests? What native and third-party integrations are required?

Customer Management – How do you manage the customer support process from allocation of cases, through different stages to closure?

Knowledge Sharing – How can you build, manage and share customer support resources between the team and with customers directly?

Monitoring Progress – How do you track interactions, collaborate with colleagues, and monitor the performance of the support team?

Customer Feedback – How do you want to capture customer feedback and satisfaction of the support service?

Within the Supermums Consultancy Skills course, we provide a full business analysis questionnaire for Service Cloud and non-functional requirements with a presentation deck and a training session on how to deliver it alongside the technical considerations. If you are worried about what questions to ask, then check out our course.

Here are five of the favourite questions you don't want to miss but there are loads more functional and non-functional requirement questions that you want to include in your questionnaire.

- What are their different products, services and customers, are their multiple customer support teams and where are their teams and customers located, globally? This will influence how many different project life cycles you will need to deliver e.g., multiple discovery workshops through to training sessions and also whether global influences are relevant such as languages and currency considerations.
- What are the pain points and key benefits they want to derive from Salesforce as a service support team from different points of view – as an organisation, a team and individually?
- How would the company measure the ROI of the Salesforce investment and how can this be measured? What are the baseline stats now and what do they want them to be in the future. It can be useful to have some example indicators here to share in case they

aren't sure. For example, reduction in cases created, reduction in case closure time, improve satisfaction score.

- How is support service performance measured? What are their key reports and dashboard requirements as they will influence how you build the system? Again, it can be useful to have some example indicators here to share in case they aren't sure. e.g., number of cases closed/open, length of time cases open, customer feedback score etc.
- What is their customer engagement and support process? Within this there will be multiple functional questions to ask and technical considerations to address, especially to discover whether the Service Cloud functionality needs extending to include Experience Cloud, native products or integration of omni-channel solutions, self-service portal, knowledge management etc. This will inevitably increase time and budget for any project.

Proposing the Right Technical Solution

As a Salesforce Administrator you will want to understand the different scenarios and technical solutions to propose to a client during the business analysis session.

Download our Service Cloud technical tests from the Book

Resources page to check your knowledge around a Service Cloud implementation and get clear on what scenarios to put on the table during the business analysis workshop.

SCAN ME

Thank you to SharinPix for sponsoring this chapter. SharinPix is the proud winner of many App Demo Jams that showcase their product.

SharinPix enables pro photo usage for your users by giving you access to a business-oriented image toolbox and unlimited photo storage at a fixed cost. This toolbox enables you to access all the image features you've ever dreamed of plus various components to build the perfect user experience. This means you no longer need to leave Salesforce to edit, resize, annotate or watermark images. You can also work offline from your mobile device to snap pictures, dictate comments, scan docs and fill in offline forms based on a PDF.

BUSINESS ANALYSIS FOR E-MARKETING

Within this chapter we give a high-level overview of what to consider during the e-marketing discovery process.

Typically, an e-marketing implementation will include the following high-level requirements:

Subscriber acquisition – what are the different ways to acquire subscribers and invite them to receive marketing emails? What is the volume of subscribers?

Customer engagement – how are subscribers categorised or segmented and how do you engage with them via e-communications. What is the type and frequency of comms?

Data integrity – what are the most important fields for data input and categorisation and how do you maintain data quality and duplicates?

Email scheduling – how many different team members are involved in scheduling emails and how do they want to manage scheduling of e-communications?

Consent management – what is the process for managing marketing consent and preferences amongst different acquisition channels and where is your source of truth?

Within the Supermums Consultancy Skills course, we provide a full business analysis questionnaire for contact management and e-marketing requirements with a presentation deck and a training session on how to deliver it alongside the technical considerations. If you are worried about what questions to ask, then check out our course.

Here are five of our favourite questions you don't want to miss but there are loads more functional and non-functional requirement questions you may want to include in your questionnaire.

- Who are their different stakeholders? What is the volume of these contacts, what information do they collect about them, how do they categorise or segment them in contacts and get them opted into marketing emails? Where are they located and is language a consideration?
- What are the pain points? Also, what are the key benefits they want to derive from Salesforce as a marketing team from different points of view – as an organisation, a team and individually?
- How would the company measure the ROI of the Salesforce/e-marketing investment and how can this be measured? What are the baseline stats now and what do they want it to be in the future. It can be useful to have

some example indicators here to share in case they aren't sure. For example, increase in subscribers, improved open rates, increase in sales, increase in conversion rate.

- How is marketing performance measured? What are their key reports and dashboard requirements as they will influence how you build the system? Again, it can be useful to have some example indicators here to share in case they aren't sure. e.g., number of subscribers, open rates, subscriber retention, volume of sales.
- What is their subscriber nurture process? What are the frequency and style of emails being sent to people and how will this be managed centrally by the team? How do people consent and managing their preferences via different subscriber channels and what is the source of truth?

Proposing the Right Technical Solution

As a Salesforce Administrator/business analyst you will want to understand the different scenarios and technical solutions to propose to a client during the business analysis session.

Download our e-marketing technical tests from the Book Resources page to check your knowledge around e-marketing implementation and get clear on what scenarios to put on the table during the business analysis workshop.

SCAN ME

Thank you to 360 SMS for sponsoring this chapter. In cracking the SMS conversions code, 360 SMS helps customers understand the ROI that can be generated through using integrated communication tools and share how companies can grow their revenue.

The 360 SMS app is a communication suite built natively on Salesforce, facilitating customer communications via SMS, WhatsApp, LINE, CTI dialler, Facebook, Instagram and WeChat.

BUSINESS ANALYSIS FOR FUNDRAISING

Within this chapter we give a high-level overview of what to consider during the fundraising discovery process.

Typically, a fundraising implementation will include the following high level requirements:

Online donations – do you have one-off, recurring or multiple transactions and which integrated payment solution will meet their needs?

Acknowledging donors – how do you categorise and manage donors into levels and acknowledge their contributions?

Managing funders – how do you nurture and secure different types and levels of funders through the fundraising pipeline and how do you maximise the Non-profit Success Pack (NPSP) functionality?

Monitoring progress – how do you schedule and log activities, collaborate with colleagues and monitor the performance of the fundraising team?

Funding to finance management – how do you manage and/or integrate funding secured with the financial management systems?

Within the Supermums Consultancy Skills course we provide a full business analysis questionnaire for fundraising, online payment and non-functional requirements with a presentation deck and a training session on how to deliver it alongside the technical considerations. If you are worried about what questions to ask, check out our course.

Here are five of our favourite questions you don't want to miss but there are loads more functional and non-functional requirement questions that you may want to include in your questionnaire.

- What are their different fundraising streams and fundraising teams; and where are their teams and customers located, globally? This will influence how many different project life cycles you will need to deliver e.g., multiple discovery workshops through to training sessions and also whether global influences are relevant such as languages and currency.
- What are the pain points and key benefits they want to derive from Salesforce as a fundraising team from different points of view – as an organisation, a team and individually?
- How would the company measure the ROI of the Salesforce investment? What are the baseline stats now and what do they want them to be in the future. It can

be useful to have some example indicators here to share in case they aren't sure. For example, increase in online donations, increase in donor retention, increase in recurring donations.

- How is fundraising performance measured? What are their key reports and dashboard requirements as they will influence how you build the system? Again, it can be useful to have some example indicators here to share in case they aren't sure. E.g., fundraising achievements vs targets, number of net new donors a month, number of one off to recurring donor conversions.
- What is their funder/donor nurture process? Within this there will be multiple functional questions to ask and technical considerations to address, especially to discover whether the NPSP /fundraising functionality needs extending to include integration of online payment solutions, event management, or financial management solutions. This will inevitably increase time and budget for any project.

Proposing the Right Technical Solution

As a Salesforce Administrator/business analyst you will want to understand the different scenarios and technical solutions to propose to a client during the business analysis session.

Download our fundraising technical tests from the Book Resources page to check your knowledge around a fundraising implementation and get clear on what scenarios to put on the table during the business analysis workshop.

SCAN ME

Thank you to Aedon Accounting for sponsoring this chapter. Aedon Accounting is an easy-to-use Salesforce financial package. Integrating your finance system and CRM on Salesforce is efficient. All your data is in one place. There are no integrations. Standard dashboards deliver all your reporting with no need for complicated Excel. Use native Salesforce features to automate the mundane, approvals, escalations, etc. Implementation is quick - in less than one VAT quarter - and training is minimal. Aedon has full finance functionality: multi-company, recurring invoices, revenue recognition, bank feeds, UK and Irish VAT.

CAREER PROGRESSION

DEFINING YOUR CAREER AMBITIONS

Once you feel you have mastered the skills of a Salesforce Administrator you might want to explore your Salesforce career ambitions.

One way to advance your career to build your confidence, land a job, or get a promotion is to really carve out your niche in the Salesforce arena.

The first step is to understand what you are passionate about and what makes you shine when you talk about it.

What Could your Salesforce Niche be?

- **Industry related** Salesforce focuses on selling its products into certain industry verticals. Do you have relevant experience and a passion for working in certain industries and would you like to focus on this niche?
- **Product related** – do you have a passion for a certain Salesforce product in which you want to become an expert? Do you want to immerse yourself in the product and all the third-party extensions, be it Service Cloud,

Sales Cloud, Marketing Cloud, CPQ, MuleSoft and beyond?

- **Skill related** – do you have a passion for admin, automation, business analysis, project management, DevOps, training, coding, or architecture for example and do you want to become a champion for one of these skills and share your passion and skills?
- **Mission related** – do you have a passion for championing and supporting certain members of the community with similar backgrounds? For example, equality groups, locality, or industry customers, just like I did by launching Supermums.

Once you've identified your Salesforce niche, you want to build your confidence in this area to feel like you have the authority to shine and speak. Seek feedback from people you have worked with and start asking for LinkedIn testimonials, so they are publicly available for people to see. Appreciate and accept the great feedback, to boost your confidence and develop your believe in yourself.

How to Build your Confidence and Gain Traction in your Salesforce Niche

- Complete any relevant certifications that back up your expertise.

- Start to document your winning formula, strategy or tips that you could share with others.
- Mentor others who are learning this area.
- Start to present on this topic within internal meetings or training sessions.
- Share some of your top tips on social media and see people's reactions.

Once you feel comfortable and believe that you have something to share with others, it's time to step it up. Put together a one-page profile that summarises your 'speaker' topics, your background, testimonials and your credentials and use this to leverage new opportunities.

How to Amplify your Personal Brand in the Salesforce Arena

- You could apply for a role or ask to become the internal specialist or head of department in your niche.
- Put yourself forward to speak at user group events.
- Offer to co-host a user group.
- Submit speaker sessions for Salesforce Community events.
- Write articles to submit them to existing blogs.
- Start your own blog and write regularly.
- Put yourself forward as a guest speaker on podcasts.
- Start your own podcast show.

- Launch a YouTube tutorial channel and create YouTube tutorials.

Find the medium that works for you and the one you are most comfortable working within. Seek training on how to present or how do optimise a blog or YouTube channel if you decide to launch a medium on your own. It's time to step out of your comfort zone but you don't have to do it alone. Make sure you are surrounded by experts who can help you on your way.

Most importantly, you want to enjoy it and to shine. So, focus on your zone of genius and become a 'Super Salesforce Professional'!

DEFINING YOUR CAREER PATH

When you start as a Salesforce Administrator it's great to have a progression plan with your employer that outlines your learning plan with roles and responsibilities that sets out how a promotion and salary increase can take place. As a Salesforce professional, you should always be learning, acquiring new skills, and developing your potential. There are different career tracks you could take, and we want to help you plan out your journey to learning and earning more.

From starting out as a Salesforce Administrator there are four different career paths you could go down.

If you enjoy managing the system and users day to day and doing the technical work, you can progress your career as a Salesforce Administrator and advance to CRM manager.

If you enjoy gathering new requirements, designing new solutions and implementing the CRM roadmap, you might want to pursue a Salesforce consultant role.

If you enjoy the technical side of the job and want to advance your skills with code, you can carve out your career as a Salesforce developer.

If you have a background in marketing and enjoy

maximising customer communications and ROI, you might want to expand your knowledge with Marketing Cloud and progress your career as a Marketing Cloud consultant.

Download our free guide on the '4 Career Paths of a Salesforce Administrator' from our Book Resources page. It covers the job expectations, salary, skills, and training needed to progress as a CRM system manager, consultant, developer or Marketing Cloud professional.

SCAN ME

What Should YOU Do Next?

Find the right Salesforce course for you.

At Supermums we deliver a range of Salesforce courses that provide structure, quality and level of accountability which generates the motivation you need to succeed. Find out more about our training courses and get started today!

Looking for a Job or to Hire a Candidate?

Supermums also has an award-winning recruitment company. We specialise in placing candidates in flexible roles within the

Salesforce ecosystem. Talk to us if you're looking for your next role or are an employer looking to find the right candidate.

CONCLUSION

After running through all of the different roles of *Become a Super Salesforce Administrator*, you should now feel reassured rather than overwhelmed by the prospect. Everyone reading this book will be on their own journey of learning and at a different stage in their Salesforce career, so don't worry if you haven't mastered everything just yet. The important thing is that you are learning; learning how to do things or checking that what you are doing is right. That makes you amazing. This capacity to appraise, renew and reshape how you deliver something if you feel it needs a new or better approach will make you a fantastic Salesforce Administrator.

Whatever stage you're at, this book should have answered a lot of questions for you, and possiblyraised some too! We hope it has helped you appraise your current level of knowledge and supported you to start formulating a strategy for being a Salesforce Administrator in a confident way.

You can use the book and the online resources I've linked to as a trusty action plan to keep you focused on what you need to do. Plus, you can carve out a plan for your career to ignite your motivation. What experience do you want to gain? What skills do you want to develop? Which areas do you want to specialise in? If you can master these skills with confidence, the world is your oyster and there should be nothing stopping you from ramping up your salary and accelerating your career progression.

If you would like to share any lightbulb moments or benefits you feel the book has given you, please do leave a review and/or share it with anyone you feel might enjoy it. I would love to hear your thoughts.

If you think you might want further support to advance your skills and confidence in your Salesforce career, there are two ways that I, and Supermums, can support you going forward. First, you can sign up to the Supermums consultancy skills course content, which offers you further in-depth training and mentoring on business analysis, change management and Agile PM, as well as more intensive BA information for the different Salesforce projects and areas covered in this book. At Supermums we can also support companies to hire emerging and experienced Salesforce talent and upskill individuals with Salesforce skills. So, let us know if we can help in any way.

Second, you could hire me as a strategic adviser to support the Salesforce team, the executive sponsor and CoE team within your organisation to help them understand how to lead a Salesforce project with confidence. I do this through delivering coaching and training on the core principles and areas covered within this book. See the back of the book for details.

ACKNOWLEDGEMENTS

I would like to extend my gratitude to the sponsors who support Supermums and, in some cases, have also contributed to the content of this book.

Box

Improved Apps

EXAH

CUBE84

CloudGaia

Nebula Consulting

Frankly Solutions

CONVAYER

Rocketphone.Ai

Hubbl

Gearset

Processity

SharinPix

Validity

360SMS

Cloud Alley

Pipelaunch

Sweep

Aedon Accounting

Validity

360SMS

INTRODUCING SUPERMUMS

Supermums helps people to launch and accelerate their Salesforce career in three main ways:

- Free educational events – Supermums runs a series of events throughout the year, which can include peer certification study groups, ISV demo jams and experience weeks.
- Training courses – Supermums is a Salesforce authorised training provider. We deliver flexible public and in-house Salesforce training courses with certified instructors across EMEA and USA time zones.

Talent supply and recruitment services – Supermums can supply emerging and experienced talent to fill a range of permanent or contract roles to help implement or manage Salesforce.

The above services are open to everyone. Proceeds from the sale of this book will be reinvested into a bursary fund to offer free or discounted training places to women who have suffered from domestic violence and want to regain their financial independence.

As a social enterprise, we are passionate about our mission of supporting mothers and tackling the following agendas:

- Reducing the gender pay gap
- Supporting women returners
- Increasing the number of women in tech
- Addressing the digital skills gap

Companies and people can support our mission through hiring our talent, sponsoring our educational content (including this book) and volunteering as ambassadors, mentors and trainers. We currently have over 180 volunteers worldwide that support us.

Find out more about Supermums by visiting our Book Resources page.

SCAN ME

ABOUT THE AUTHOR

Heather Black started out as an accidental admin and then upskilled to become a freelance Salesforce consultant in 2011. She is eight-times certified, a change management and NLP practitioner and holds both a diploma in

business analysis practice and a foundation in Agile DSDM project management.

Heather ran a Salesforce consultancy for ten years, winning the EMEA Salesforce Consulting Partner of the Year award. During this time, she oversaw over 700 projects with 350 customers and was a member of the Salesforce EMEA Partner Advisory Board.

Since 2020, she has focused on training and advising executive sponsors and Salesforce professionals on how to lead digital transformation and Salesforce projects, by teaching them essential skills via the Supermums Consultancy Skills course while also providing one-to-one mentoring.

She is the founder of Supermums, a global social enterprise that helps to launch and accelerate the careers of women within the Salesforce ecosystem through providing a training and recruitment service. Since 2016, Supermums has supported over 1,500 trainees and more than 300 employers to find super talent.

Heather is a coveted Golden Hoodie winner, due to her efforts championing women in tech, and was recognised in the 100 Most Influential Women in Tech by *Computer Weekly* and in the Tech Women 100 Awards by *We Are Tech Women*, amongst other accolades.

She writes content and speaks regularly at Salesforce events and user groups on topics related to the A to Z of how to lead a Salesforce project, how to be a super Salesforce consultant and how to accelerate your career as a woman in tech with the ambitious women mindset. She has presented for audiences of over 10,000 including at Dreamforce, Salesforce World Tour London, Salesforce World Tour Manchester, Dreamforce to You London, Marie Claire and Sales- force Partner Events, MERC and Chase 25.

Introducing Supermums

www.supermums.org

www.facebook.com/supermumsglobal/

www.linkedin.com/company/supermumsglobal/

www.instagram.com/supermumscareers

Made in United States
North Haven, CT
04 November 2026

21771220R00127